Praise for *Radical Dharma*

"It is rather astonishing that the Black tradition of continuous and endless enlightenment in this country produces its prophets as if bad laws, discrimination, horrors of financial inequality and so on, do not exist to blight the way. No wonder one often imagines the ancestors laughing. This is a book to grow on, to deepen over, to partner with. We are on a magnificent journey of liberation, every moment we are alive in this odd place that has yet to awaken to itself. And we are always, generation to generation, ready to travel. How cool is this?"

—Alice Walker, American novelist and poet

"*Radical Dharma* is a clear, honest testimony of the heart from three provocative leaders of our time. You may not always see things just as they do (I didn't) or even feel like you fully understand it all (again, I didn't) but that makes it even more important to read."

—Sharon Salzberg, author of *Lovingkindness* and *Real Happiness*

"*Radical Dharma* is both radical ... and courageous. The authors build upon the growing understanding of the connection between personal and societal liberation. *Radical Dharma* unflinchingly turns this lens to this most challenging and critical nexus of racism and white supremacy. We whites on a spiritual path are lovingly challenged to get our butts off the mat, understanding that our personal liberation is impossible while we unconsciously enjoy the privileges of our skin color. Those in pain and enraged from the brutalities of oppression are lovingly challenged to get that we will never create a liberated society without attending to our own liberation. This is not an 'easy' book. Just like a Zen koan, *Radical Dharma* asks provocative questions rather than prescriptive answers, questions that unsettle, questions that challenge some of our most precious assumptions. Through personal stories and dialogue, we are invited on a powerful journey of spiritual and political awakening. Take the invitation!"

—Robert Gass, EdD, cofounder, Rockwood Leadership Institute and Social Transformation Project

"This is a moving and crucial book for anyone interested in the flourishing of the dharma in the West. Read it, sit with it and then get off the cushion and do something radical to make a difference."

—Cheryl A. Giles, Francis Greenwood Peabody Senior Lecturer on Pastoral Care and Counseling at Harvard Divinity School, coeditor of *The Arts of Contemplative Care: Pioneering Voices in Buddhist Chaplaincy and Pastoral Work,* and Tibetan Buddhist practitioner

"*Radical Dharma* is a powerful and vulnerable circle held by three Dharma practitioners who are people of color. It is a beautiful and rare invitation to listen to how each transformed their pain. Some of this is familiar: no one sees me because of my weight. And some of this, for white people, will be new: What does it look like to truly sit with the pain caused by racism in your body? *Radical Dharma* demands that we step into the circle and ask: How do we restore our humanity? How do we transform ourselves and the world? In this book, Rev. angel Kyodo williams has created a powerful circle of truth around race and reconciliation. Sit, participate, and be broken open and transformed. Understand how the system of racism has traumatized all of us and how we need to heal individually and collectively."

—Marianne Manilov, cofounder, Engage Network

"As informed and informative as it is thoughtful and thought-provoking. An absolutely timely and substantive contribution to our current national dialogue on racial justice and the dangerous rise of white supremacy in our national politics."

—*Midwest Book Review*

Also by Rev. angel Kyodo williams

Being Black: Zen and the Art of Living with Fearlessness and Grace

radicaldharma.org

RADICAL DHARMA

TALKING RACE, LOVE, AND LIBERATION

Rev. angel Kyodo williams

Lama Rod Owens

with Jasmine Syedullah, PhD

North Atlantic Books
Berkeley, California

Published by North Atlantic Books
Berkeley, California

Cover concept by Rev. angel Kyodo williams
Cover art by Jasmine Hromjak
Cover and book design by Jasmine Hromjak
Printed in the United States of America

Radical Dharma: Talking Race, Love, and Liberation is sponsored and published by the Society for the Study of Native Arts and Sciences (dba North Atlantic Books), an educational nonprofit based in Berkeley, California, that collaborates with partners to develop cross-cultural perspectives, nurture holistic views of art, science, the humanities, and healing, and seed personal and global transformation by publishing work on the relationship of body, spirit, and nature.

North Atlantic Books' publications are available through most bookstores. For further information, call 800-733-3000 or visit our website at www.northatlanticbooks.com.

Library of Congress Cataloging-in-Publication Data
Names: Williams, Angel Kyodo, author. | Owens, Rod, author. | Syedullah, Jasmine, author.
Title: Radical Dharma : talking race, love, and liberation / Rev. angel Kyodo Williams, Lama Rod Owens, Jasmine Syedullah, Ph.D.
Description: Berkeley, California : North Atlantic Books, [2016]
Identifiers: LCCN 2016015115 | ISBN 9781623170981 (paperback)
Subjects: LCSH: Racism—Religious aspects—Buddhism. | Racism—United States. | Social conflict—Religious aspects--Buddhism. | Toleration—Religious aspects—Buddhism. | Equality—Religious aspects—Buddhism. | BISAC: SOCIAL SCIENCE / Discrimination & Race Relations. | RELIGION / Buddhism / General (see also PHILOSOPHY / Buddhist). | SOCIAL SCIENCE / Gay Studies.
Classification: LCC BQ4570.R3 W55 2016 | DDC 294.3089/00973—dc23
LC record available at https://lccn.loc.gov/2016015115

5 6 7 8 KPC 20 19 18
Printed on recycled paper

North Atlantic Books is committed to the protection of our environment. We partner with FSC-certified printers using soy-based inks and print on recycled paper whenever possible.

EDITOR'S NOTE

REV. ANGEL KYODO WILLIAMS SENSEI, Lama Rod Owens, and Jasmine Syedullah, PhD, traveled between Brooklyn, NY, Atlanta, GA, Boston, MA, and Berkeley, CA, to facilitate the long-overdue conversation about how people can remain accountable to social transformation while facing the truths of racism and privilege, whether doing inner work or working in the social sphere. These open-community conversations—in which the Black prophetic tradition meets the wisdom of the Dharma—are a compassionate response to the racial injustice running rampant in the United States. In particular, the underlying systemic, state-sanctioned violence and oppression that have persisted against Black people since the slave era was brought to national attention by the killings of Michael Brown and Eric Garner. Their deaths set in motion a new iteration of a Black-centered movement for liberation, the achievement of which we believe must be articulated by and inextricably linked to an embodied personal liberation.

Radical Dharma: Talking Race, Love, and Liberation follows in the same prophetic tradition as Cornel West and bell hooks' *Breaking Bread: Insurgent Black Intellectual Life* and is meant to ignite the much-needed conversation about the legacy of racial and structural injustice, both in self-identified dharma communities and in the United States, to move its people, together, toward healing and liberation.

It is our duty to fight for our freedom.
It is our duty to win.
We must love each other and support each other.
We have nothing to lose but our chains.

—ASSATA SHAKUR, from *Assata: An Autobiography*
   and refrain of the Black Lives Matter movement

CONTENTS

PREFACE: A LINEAGE OF INSURGENCE

by Rev. angel Kyodo williams, Sensei

Radical Dharma is insurgence rooted in love, and all that love of self and others implies. It takes self-liberation to its necessary end by moving beyond personal transformation to transcend dominant social norms and deliver us into collective freedom.

—Rev. angel Kyodo williams, Sensei

WHY THIS BOOK? WHY NOW?

If you're like me, aware of the urgency of the moment—that is to say it has always been urgent, but we are increasingly aware of it—there will be something both strikingly hopeful and terribly dissatisfying about this book.

I think that's the right place to be.

On the one hand, it seeks to be responsive to this moment in history, the unique precipice of the cultural ledge we're peering over. We even pressed for the publication of the book to happen well before the 2016 presidential election rather than right in the thick of it. We foresee an increasing collective anxiety about transitioning from the first Black U.S. president. Whether you agreed or disagreed with the sum total of the Obama presidency and where it sat on the political spectrum—liberal or centrist or dipping further to the right—the pure optics of it is that it returns us to a white-led country. For many of us, way too soon. There is an undeniable psycho-emotional loss and processing of grief that must occur. (Just as I'm sure there is an equal sense of relief to be experienced by those who have been vehemently and subtly disturbed by a Black man in that role.)

On the other hand, true to the contemplative roots of our training and practice, it calls for a degree of reflection, opening questions at a time that feels insistently in need of answers. It calls for restraint. I even dare say it calls for pause.

We recognize that the conversations shared don't offer answers; in fact, we don't even think these *are* the conversations. As in: though they are presented in conversation form, they are merely an on-ramp. An on-ramp to what? To *the* conversations. To the conversations that must be had in order to create the conditions for creative solutions to emerge from the collective. For that to happen, we must actually experience ourselves as a collective above and beyond the convenient but insufficient labels we have projected forth and hidden behind for too long: liberal, progressive, ally, friend.

It asks us to not only look but also *do* the inner work that has been underemphasized. For too long we've been beholden to a set of surface feelings, organizing around ideas and beliefs about what it means to be a good person or create good society. These efforts at good behavior and pursuit of good policies have proven to be no match for the deep embeddedness of what is the foundation of, and has been intricately woven throughout, every facet, institution, and relationship of the United States and the psyche of its inhabitants: the racialization of people and its underlying presupposition—the superiority of white-skinned peoples. A direct requirement of maintaining that position has always been and continues to be the inferiority of Black people.

In the civil rights era, Christians and other people of faith were called upon to look into their hearts to know the right side to be on, the right thing to do. Indeed, they found righteousness there. But they mostly found a piteous empathy that supposed the greater, more powerful, more better people should bestow fairness upon the other, lesser ones.

But neither Christianity nor any other faith alone can deliver us into a systems analysis that can unravel the massive entanglement that white supremacy is in every aspect of how we think, feel, dream, and act toward ourselves and others based on our perception of their place in the social order. Rank is still the evolutionarily Neanderthal mode by which our social and religious cultures are organized, and it systematically undermines every enlightened impulse we have.

Thus, every institution, every organization, every culture, every community, every belief system, every frame of mind we currently have that organizes itself and operates within the social order imposed by the rank of white-centered racialization is ill-equipped to meet the complexity of structures built from the ground up to elevate some on the backs of others. Its centralized location and grand projections compel us all to believe the evidence of the outcome as proving the original supposition: that whites are better than Blacks, and Blacks are worse than anyone. Whether one consciously aspires to it or not, there's no argument to be had here, nothing to defend. Unless you simply believe that Black, indigenous, and people of color are inferior, the evidence of the system and its efficacy is the collective state of the diminished position of these peoples throughout the entire western hemisphere and the Global South.

It is our duty to fight for our freedom.

But there is an insurgence here.

Rather than continue to accept a second-, third-, or any lesser-class position, the movements for Black liberation being advanced by non-white people and their white conscious compañer@s are naming, resisting, and rising against white supremacy and its many tentacles that have had a stranglehold on the humanity of all peoples. Their struggle is to be free from inequity, oppression, domination, and subjugation. Its pursuit is social liberation and the collective realization of truly just, sustainable, and equitable societies.

Simultaneously, Buddhist thought has positioned itself for millennia to analyze the complex system of the construct known to us as the self. It has as its goal the unearthing of the bonds that tether us as individuals to seemingly endless cycles on micro and macro levels of unnecessary suffering. It proposes practices that seek to expose and cut through the unwholesome roots of needless suffering. It heralds the ever--present possibility of personal liberation and the resulting resilience, depth of capacity, peace of mind, strength of heart, and wise action.

It is our duty to win.

THE WEIGHT OF FREEDOM

The sheer weight of the task of unraveling a massive social-habit pattern of and addiction to violence and injustice cannot be underestimated. It comes with the requisite and convenient forgetfulness about historic transgressions of such enormity and persistence they boggle the mind. It proves daunting at the least, stunningly and increasingly complex throughout and at its edges, destructive on mental, physical, material, and psycho-spiritual levels. Even as the effort is meant to liberate, its current methodology, though evolved substantively by way of historic learning and ancestral wisdom, was forged within the very same constructs it seems to undermine: orientations toward divide and conquer, competition over cooperation, power over rather than with us and them.

We must love each other and support each other.

I have been struck by the examples of a national leader whose social-media post in response to people's suggestions for self-care at a time of great external intensity was to be upset: "I don't have time for y'all's self-care bullshit. We are out here facing real shit. Keep that to yourself" is how I read it.

To be fair, not all of the leaders and practitioners of the current iteration of movements for Black liberation abide within these frameworks. In fact, it has been my bearing witness to a vision that sees beyond the constructs that the forces of oppression seek to contain us all within that most inspires this writing. As a written work, *Radical Dharma* seeks to recognize, reflect, and amplify the searing truth to the power spoken from the inspiring leaders, national and local, who give voice and shape to the contours of this emerging movement. It seeks to provide a still point of reflection on deeper questions that live in people's hearts even when these questions don't survive news cycles and social-media feeds.

For, until our capital-V vision for liberation gives way to an accessible, translatable, adaptable yet rigorous praxis at meaningful scale—one that can match in energy and rebound through rhythm from the sustained stress the structures of oppression are designed to burden our minds, our bodies, and our hearts with—we cannot uproot those forces.

As Bruce Lee famously said, "Under duress, we do not rise to our expectations, but fall to our level of training." Hundreds of years of living in a context designed by pillagers of the land and captors of people—without sufficient intervention—naturally establishes the curriculum of the training to which we fall. Our methodologies are forged within the default mindset of colonization, capitalism-as-religion, corporation-as-demigod, domination over people and planet, winner take all, rape and plunder as spoils of victory, human and natural resources taken as objects of subjugation to the land-owning, resource-controlling, very, very privileged few.

I am stilled by the growing number of stories speaking of the toll that sustained resistance to great force without sufficient tools for resilience has taken. Even when we are conscious about how these structures can manifest in our work, without appropriate training of skill and depth our strategies for coping play the well-intended flip side of the destruction card: suppression, depression, diversion, martyrdom, and simply taking it until there's no room left in our bodies to contain the force of destruction, so that like the dis-ease it is, it turns inward against us. Most distressing is when conscious communities cannot provide support because the depth of suffering is not known as was the case in the suicide of the young Black activist MarShawn McCarrell II. Without practices of self-witness that exist in dynamic balance with the will to liberate the collective, the level of suffering we may bear in exchange is perhaps not even known to ourselves.

We have nothing to lose but our chains.

Radical Dharma brings a megaphone and a spotlight to these pursuits for liberation, amplifying their virtues and casting a light into the shadows that can overwhelm their intentions. But don't be fooled ... even when the words point to particular groups of people or communities—whether Black, brown, white, Buddhist, queer, margin, or mainstream—*Radical Dharma* is not about subject and object, practitioner and observer. It's about liberation. It speaks through these individual identities into the whole. One abiding theory that emerges from the practice of a radical dharma that presents itself is that you should know this, attend to that, be aware of these things, but you must do them for your liberation, not mine.

The book situates every person who claims the lineage of liberation—whether personal or social—within a tradition of radical social transformation, both as bodies moving against the stream and as bodies that bear the wisdom, witness, and wounds of intersecting and overlapping structures of violence, policing, and erasure.

Every body bears these wounds, so when we bear witness to suffering, we bear the wisdom—prophetic wisdom—of liberation from that suffering. And we bear it together.

LINEAGE: TOUCHING THE EARTH, MAKING ROOM FOR EVERYONE

The 2,600-year-old teaching of the historical Buddha has its roots in India. From the very earliest days, the various traditions his teachings inspired have been historically governed by lineage as a matter of spiritual, cultural, and even familial importance.

In the West, teachings have transcended their geographic, religious, and cultural origins. Having landed squarely in the midst of a culture increasingly obsessed with breaking from tradition, deconstructing, and re-inventing everything—which could be seen as appropriation—lineage-as-authenticity begs new questioning: How do we make visible those who have been marginalized while respecting the deep roots of these practices? How can we confidently access, translate, and share this deeply valuable wisdom within different communities and cultures without parsing out what doesn't easily fit our comfort zones? How do we avoid watering down the deeply transformative nature of these teachings in the name of creating access?

On the one hand, we can and do point back to the historical Buddha as validation of our rightful place in a line of teachings passed down directly from person to person. On the other hand, where do those of us who have had our ancestral lineages forcibly erased fit in? What if our known lineages are not proud ones?

Finally, when access to teachings are hindered by bias and discrimination or the dynamics of power, shame, and ignorance, who bears witness to the essential nature of such teachings that transcends color, class, and caste of all kinds?

ISTANBUL, FEBRUARY 22, 2016

INTRODUCTION: ENTER HERE

RADICAL CHALLENGE

by Rev. angel Kyodo williams, Sensei

RAD·ik·uhl: relating to or affecting the fundamental nature of something; far-reaching or thorough. (derived from radix—going to the root).

DAR·ma: universal Truth.

The Black Radical Tradition is foundational to people who are not Black, for it is only with the liberation of Black people that humanity can be freed from its chains of oppression, just as Black people cannot be liberated while humanity is in chains.[1]

WHY RADICAL?

We live in a culture in which our first reaction and response to something we don't like or are uncomfortable with is to want to change it. We want it to go away…so we want to change it. What we have not learned to do is to give ourselves the space and time to simply observe it as it is, to make friends with it.

---

[1] "BROC Statement." The Black Radical Tradition Conference. Accessed March 25, 2016. http://www.theblackradicaltradition.org/statement2/.

As powerfully painful as that may be—with all due respect to Gandhi—we can no longer afford to just be the change. We actually have to be the transformation, which is to say we have to transcend the form, the construct that we find ourselves in.

The only way we can do that is to observe the construct that we're in instead of trying to tinker with it right away with the same blind spots that we came to the problem with. Immediately, we get out our tools, and you know the saying that when you have a hammer, the whole world looks like a nail? And so we start hammering away, but we've exhausted the hammer and require new tools. We can't see that if we won't observe what is, because we're trying so hard to get away from it. We're trying to evade the grief and trauma of our own racism and our internalized racism and our continuous perpetuation of racism and classism and other forms of oppression on ourselves and others every single day. Every single one of us. Just like in our personal lives. We've often had some kind of floor-falling-out-beneath-us experience, and some of us get it and some of us don't. If we don't respond to each opportunity that opens up, we need greater falls from higher heights before we look at ourselves in the mirror and say, "Oh! I've actually called this moment to me to recognize that I need to make some kind of fundamental shift."

As a society, we are in danger of needing larger and larger social wake-up calls and shocks to the system. At a socio-global scale, this translates into more strident demagogues, more desperate and deeply fundamentalist takeovers, massive cultural disruption and human displacement, more vicious, faceless wars, and literally larger openings in the earth to swallow us up.

A UNION OF IDEALS:
THE GREATER SUM OF PARTS

By the grace of many Eastern traditions, teachers, and ancestors, white Western dharma communities have at their disposal profoundly liberating teachings and practices that have the power to sever at their very root the destructive behaviors and thought processes that we inherit by way of our birth into human bodies. But we have largely refused to turn the great light of this collective wisdom of mind, body, and spirit onto the systems that bestow unearned privilege, position, and profit. In so doing, we diminish the precious truths we have chosen to steward. We must take a stand.

Movements for Black liberation cast their bodies into resisting the systems and instruments of oppression. Our bodies take the shape of, and thus illuminate, the contours of the most insidious force of systematic dehumanization and destruction ever imagined, one which has led the global community into a downward spiral of self-annihilation. Our insistent march exemplifies a grace and forbearance that humbles and inspires direct confrontation with the truth, widening the path of justice toward liberation for all people. We are propelled by the essential human compulsion for freedom, but we can also be driven by centuries of pain and carrying a burden greater than people should have ever known. Our healing cannot wait until the structures acquiesce, are dismantled, or come undone. We must take a seat.

Each community possesses, as Gandhi offered, a piece of the truth, of Dharma. When we seek the embodiment of these truths, giving ourselves permission to be more honest, more healed, more whole, more complete—when we become radical—neither the path of solely inward-looking liberation nor the pursuit of an externalized social liberation prevails; rather a third space, as-yet-unknown, emerges. It is a radical dharma. And it is ours.

Lama Rod, Jasmine, and I bridge these communities. We cast our bodies into the third space that emerges when radically inhabiting the two: the inner *and* outer paths toward liberation. We do it out of necessity, choice, for healing, and the unwavering faith that comes from having touched and been touched by the Truth. We offer our own truth and have brought forth the truth and inquiries of others that are stretching to bridge these terrains. The terrains are expressed as dichotomies only because we have not yet completed our work, but we know in our bodies we must one day abide there. Inner and outer. Personal and social. Love and justice. Liberation.

To inhabit radical as an ideal is to commit to going beyond one's familiar or even chosen terrain. It avails you to what you weren't willing to see, which is the place Truth resides.

To embody that truth is to live beyond the limits of self-reinforcing habits, which take the narrative of the past, project it onto the future, and obscure the present, leaving us to sleepwalk in the dreamscape of other people's desires and determinations.

It is to transcend the borders erected by pain, fear, and apathy, to discover a new territory unbound by the privileges and preferences that trade freedom for familiarity and comfort but pretend they are one and the same.

Because by definition it can never be static; to be radical is to constantly live in the territory yet undiscovered, the liberation yet unknown.

NEW DHARMA, RADICAL DHARMA

It wouldn't be an overstatement to say that the discovery and assertion of Siddhartha Gautama, the historic Buddha—that every human being, irrespective of caste, race, creed, or birth has within them the potential for waking up to the ultimate nature of reality—is one of the most radically life-altering propositions for human life on and in relationship to the planet. One that we need right now.

Yet, at this time when the Dharma is needed more acutely than ever—a time when our very existence is threatened as a result of our socially embedded greed, hatred, and ignorance—its expansive potential to liberate us from suffering is in danger of being rendered impotent because it is held in subjugation to the very systems that it must thoroughly examine.

Thrust into the Western socioeconomic framework that puts profit above all and coupled with a desire to perpetuate institutional existence at the expense of illuminating reality and revealing deeper truths, the Dharma has become beholden to commodification as inescapable and *de rigueur*. Authenticity and integrity are thus compromised.

Much of what is being taught is the acceptance of a "kinder, gentler suffering" that does not question the unwholesome roots of systemic suffering and the structures that hold it in place. What is required is a new Dharma, a radical Dharma that deconstructs rather than amplifies the systems of suffering, that starves rather than fertilizes the soil of the conditions that the deep roots of societal suffering grow in. A new Dharma is one that insists we investigate not only the unsatisfactoriness of our own minds but also prepares us for the discomfort of confronting the obscurations of the society we are individual expressions of. It recognizes that the delusions of systemic oppression are not solely the domain of the individual. By design, they are seated within and reinforced by society.

We must wake up and cut through not only individual but also social ego. This is not only our potential, but we now each have it as our collective responsibility. As dharma communities—this includes people belonging to white-led, Western communities of convert Buddhists, but also next-generation yogis, Advaitins, Sikhs, and adopters of other Eastern traditions—we must also do so strategically, and with great haste.

THERE IS NO NEUTRAL

We are at a critical moment in the history of the nation, as well as within the Buddhist teaching and tradition in America. This is the "back of the bus" moment of our time. Fifty years after civil rights laws were laid down, it is clear that they were enshrined within a structure that continues to profit from anti-Black racism. The necessary bias that the system requires in order to be perpetuated has permeated our *sanghas*—our spiritual communities—and in this very moment, we are called to put aside business as usual. If you have ever wondered how you would have shown up in the face of the challenge put before white America when Rosa Parks refused to give up her seat, upending the accepted social order, now is the time you will find out. For Western-convert Buddhist America, this is the time when we will actually embody our practice and teachings, or not.

Our inability as a nation to honor the theft of these lands and the building of wealth, power, and privilege on the countless backs and graves of Black people is our most significant obstacle to being at peace with ourselves, thus with the world. The

Buddhist community is a mirror image of this deep internal conflict that arises out of a persistent resistance to playing its appropriate societal role even as we have available to us rigorous teachings to the contrary. This is a clarifying moment about who we are as individuals but also who we have been thus far as a collective of people laying claim to the teachings of the Buddha, waving the flag of wisdom and compassion all the while.

As demographics shift, ushering in increasingly racially diverse pools of seekers, this reluctance promises to be our undoing. We simply cannot engage with either the ills or promises of society if we continue to turn a blind eye to the egregious and willful ignorance that enables us to still not "get it" in so many ways. It is by no means our making, but given the culture we are emerging from and immersed in, we are responsible.

White folks' particular reluctance to acknowledge impact as a collective while continuing to benefit from the construct of the collective leaves a wound intact without a dressing. The air needed to breathe through forgiveness is smothered. Healing is suspended for all. Truth is necessary for reconciliation.

Will we express the promise of and commitment to liberation for all beings, or will we instead continue a hyper--individualized salvation model—the myth of meritocracy—that is the foundation of this country's untruth?

The work being done in Dharma communities is the same work being done by the America that wants to live up to its promise of life, liberty, and the pursuit of happiness. Collectively, we must kick the habit of racism, cultural dominance, and the upholding of oppressive systems. More poignantly, our challenge, our responsibility, our deep resounding call is to be at the forefront of this overdue evolutionary thrust forward. Why? Because we choose to position ourselves as the standard-bearers of an ethical high ground. And we have the tools and teachings to do so.

There is no neutral.

WHOSE LIBERATION?

We're in a moment in which the attention of our nation is rightfully turned to the policing of Black and brown bodies. From above, it looks like just Black and brown folks are being policed, and, while you may feel bad, at least you are free.

The policing we are witnessing is expressing itself through the State. The police force is the state institution carrying out a specific mandate. The mandate expresses an energetic need of the construct that we inhabit.

That mandate is to control Black bodies.
The need is to have the constant specter of the other.
When the other exists, it strengthens your need to belong.
Your belonging is necessary for compliance.
Your compliance maintains the system.
You are policed, too.
You are policed by your need for belonging.
Your need for belonging requires control of the other.
… Or at least the illusion of it.
You are policed through the control of my body.
You are policed, too.

Once you are aware of how you are being policed, you can begin the process of self-liberating, from the position of realizing the mutuality of our liberation rather than suffering under the delusion that you are doing something for me. There is an intimacy in that realization. And because dharma is ultimately about accepting what is, it can undermine the need for control that keeps you invested in the policing of my body, thus freeing yours.

THE SOCIAL EGO

To lean into this aspiration, you must confront the fact that "whiteness" is a social ego as void of inherent identity as the personal ego, and you have identified with it as much as your very own name, but without being willing to name it.

Just as the ego-mind is a construct that constantly reinforces itself—building structures and systems of control and developing attitudes and views that maintain its primacy and sense of solidity so that it can substantiate its validity—so, too, does this construct of whiteness. One could call it the Mind of Whiteness.

The construct has been designed so that white America—and by extension white teachers and practitioners—lives inside the prison of that small mind, such that without intentional intervention, you cannot see over the wall of the reinforcing perspectives that affirm and perpetuate the White Superiority Complex. The complex would disintegrate if the vastness of your own racial bias were illuminated. So you remain in ignorance, blind to the reality before you, which is necessary to escape the sheer anguish of how pervasive it is, how you unerringly participate and how seemingly inescapable it is.

But just as the ego-mind cannot be used to work its way out

of its own construct, so too can the Mind of Whiteness not be used to see through the veil of its own construct. On the one hand, this is where a practice that illuminates the nature of mind comes in. We are gifted with precisely the tools and methodologies needed for the project of deconstructing. But that lens of awareness must be placed outside of the construct. As a direct result of privilege, white practitioners (and teachers) have mistakenly entitled themselves to place the lens of awareness inside of whiteness, hence they are unable to see its machinations. But once we choose to live dharma in a radical way, a motivation toward complete liberation, our work can begin.

So we sit. And we feel. And we let what arises do so until the resistance is worn down, or moved through, or even seems to overwhelm us. On the other side, we see a glimmer of something that we couldn't get a handle on for our desperate need to avoid it. We begin to see Truth. And when we catch a hold of it, we can finally see the patterns of our participation in not-Truth emerge. With the clarity of a steady mind and courage of a true heart, what has always been there begins to reveal itself, emerging from behind the fog of this social ego: the Mind of Whiteness.

The white practitioners of Dharma who cannot stand firmly in acknowledging the pain caused by the decades of resistance to addressing this misalignment will be exposed as using a veneer of the dharma as mere window-dressing while milking the benefits of the system. Our wise words will land with a thud henceforth. The veil of mindfulness will be seen through as thin.

No one entity has the answer, but rather it is the willingness to offer our best, claim responsibility for our worst, and fold it all into the continuous moment-to-moment practice of simply being present to what is that promises to deliver our future.

THE SOCIAL MONASTERY

I think we've mistaken the so-called hero's journey. We believe that we can go on retreat into the monastery looking for something and get enlightened, then come out into the world as enlightened beings. But as people who are not monastics, our profound insight only comes in direct relationship with the world—the field of our practice. It is our relationship to the outer world that is the source of our awakening. We then bring the insight to the monastery where we hone and integrate it during retreat.

We bring the integration into society, into how we inhabit the environment, into our *sanghas* and communities, into how we see and treat people, and into how we let ourselves be seen. If we can do that, we come back more awake.

If the fruit of practice is not a desire to respond to the world, if it just remains in response to your own needs, "me" is all you are seeing: "I want to feel better. I want to feel like a spiritual person. I want to be seen as right. But I don't want to actually be responsible for the world that I'm in." Then you haven't yet woken up.

For myself, I couldn't theorize a radical dharma, but rather had to seek to live it through principles and practices that lean toward liberation. To embody, to use my body as the testing ground out in the world. To give myself over to a field of play in which everything is allowed to happen: examination, experimentation, failure—lots of joyous failure—into emergence. Then I step back and observe what it gives rise to. What I discover and rediscover is a third space neither contained by a dharma written in scripture nor apart from it. A New Dharma, a Radical Dharma.

BEYOND BUDDHISM

Finally, we must also be willing to release a false sense of ownership and the compulsion to capitalize in order for the Dharma to assume its rightful place as the connective tissue among the people-inhabited groups, institutions, and organizations of this societal body, infusing wisdom, compassion, and unconditional love into every breath at all levels, in all corners, and across boundaries of race, color, caste, creed, and religion.

KALEIDOSCOPE: HOW TO USE THIS BOOK

by Jasmine Syedullah, PhD

*Kaleidoscope is derived from the ancient Greek
kalos meaning "beautiful, beauty";
eidos meaning "that which is seen: form, shape";
and skope meaning "to look to, to examine"—
hence "observation of beautiful forms."*

There are a variety of lenses through which the book can be viewed. All are ways to "observe the beauty"—a means of living an increasingly more radical dharma—becoming that which we wish to see in the world.

This is a talking book. You can read it cover to cover, on your own, for yourself, or you can read it in sections, out loud, in groups. It is designed to begin the conversations we need to build new communities. To that end we invite you to consider some of the practical and political ways we chose to represent connections between our own personal liberation and collective-movement liberation.

TRANSITIONS — BEGINNINGS AND ENDINGS

Abiding in a sense of the ceremony, some sections begin with an invocation and end with a dedication of merit. These are the bits of ritual we used to frame our own dialogues and pass along to you as possible ways to engage in these conversations along with us.

STYLE AND GRACE

While race is a social construct, Blackness comes into this conversation as more than a racial category. Blackness is a distinctly political orientation to liberation that is activist, communal, and on the move! It is a generational tradition of collective resistance to white supremacy that began with the resistance of untold numbers of women, men, and children to the first glimpses of the capture and crime of New World Slavery. It is a practice of love and liberation that persists into the present day. While racial categories can be used as simple catchalls, practical ways to order and distinguish between—as W. E. B. Du Bois writes, the grosser physical differences of color, hair, and bone—in the pages that follow we capitalize the *B* in *Black* while leaving the *w* in *white* lowercase to call up the peculiar historic violence of Black racial formation. We capitalize the *B* in *Black* to call up the tradition of movement for collective liberation, both spiritual and political, that has inspired the contexts in which these conversations are unfolding. It is a tradition of liberation informed by racial categories but not limited by the kinds of violence racism imprints on our identity as Black people. We capitalize the *B* but not the *w* not to preserve or reverse the racism of white supremacy but to situate our racial identity within a radically conscious idea of history, one in which the presence of Black people in the spheres of anti-Black racism has made wholesale social transformation both inconceivable and inevitable—a way of getting past the limitations of identity politics without passing over the particular politics of our embodiment.

THE BOOK INSIDE THE BOOK

Nestled in between our essays there is a book within a book—*The Conversations* that took Radical Dharma on the road. In the course of the Radical Dharma tour, from Atlanta to Brooklyn to Boston to Berkeley, we noted how place—both physical edifice and region—shaped the tenor and texture of our conversations. While the chapters on Race, Love, and Liberation were compiled from the various locations of our Radical Dharma conversations, the chapters do not distinguish where each particular exchange took place. The tone and feel of each place was inflected by the venue, the people, the local culture and politics of the cities that hosted them. We are indebted to the communities that made these conversations so rich and full of heart. We invite you to dip into them, feel them out, and imagine how they might unfold in your own cities, in your local communities.

RETURNING TO THE CIRCLE
NOW ... AND AGAIN

Feedback from early readers suggests that it is useful to read the Preface again after you read The Conversations. The book, like a conversation, is circular in design. It begins by setting the context of the present moment, goes to the past, brings us forward and then opens space for conversation. Especially if this is new for you, returning to the context with a new set of eyes is the best way to situate what people are speaking into.

HOW'S THAT SOUND?

Nothing conveys mood like music, so relevant chapters will also be accompanied by song lyrics reflective of a combination of the authors' predilections and thematic soundtracks for the topic. Some choices will surprise and reveal the myriad influences of a generation that began to defy identity constructs and expected norms. In one work session, the Radical Dharma team took time to pay homage and watch the newly released video for Rihanna's "Bitch Better Have My Money" in which the artist kidnaps and tortures her accountant's wife, ending in Rihanna covered in blood. Girl power meets gore.

How's that for new Dharma?

SECTION I:

HOMELEAVING—WHAT WE LEFT BEHIND

REMEMBERING IN SEVEN MOVEMENTS

by Lama Rod Owens

You're mean to me.
Why must you be mean to me?
Gee, honey, it seems to me
You love to see me cryin'.

—"MEAN TO ME," AS PERFORMED BY NELL CARTER FROM
THE MUSICAL *AIN'T MISBEHAVIN*

There is rest for the weary....

—"REST FOR THE WEARY," AS PERFORMED BY SWEET
HONEY IN THE ROCK

Deliver me, O Lord, from death eternal on that fearful day,
When the heavens and the earth shall be moved,
When thou shalt come to judge the world by fire.

—"LIBERA ME," FROM TRADITIONAL REQUIEM CYCLE

HOMELEAVING

I am wondering what it has meant for me to leave home. I am
thinking of the long journeys that have taken me from one
locale to another, from one country to another; the journeys
over waters and mountains, through deserts, through places
haunted and infested, through dark places, and darkness itself. I
am thinking of wanderings from lover to lover, from glimpses
of light to memories of light, away from identity to identity

and back again; from one kind of ignorance to another. I am thinking of movement and memories of movement, always leaving and having to return again and again. Never landing in a place but somehow feeling that the place lands on me. Teetering between the past and the future. Avoiding the present because dealing with right now is sometimes the hardest thing to do.

The most difficult part of leaving is remembering what has been left, articulating the why of my leaving, regardless of how it may put me at odds with those closest to me. Yet, these have been the choices that I have most often made. I have seen them as movements.

As a young Black boy growing up in the South, my love of Black root music of traditional gospel, jazz, R&B, and soul was punctuated by a growing appetite for classical European music. The genre of music was exotic to me. By college, I had discovered the genre of concert requiems. I knew nothing of requiems or Catholicism at the time, but what moved me most about the genre was how it evolved from Eucharist services for the dead to emotional and dramatic performance works that often embodied and echoed the human struggle to make meaning of death and impermanence. Each movement of the requiem was a shift to permit the listener and performer to be creatures experiencing the suffering of old age, sickness, and death. These are the same experiences that the Buddha longed to make meaning of and which eventually motivated him to leave his home in search of transcendence from these sufferings. As I have moved in my life, I have also experienced the death of who and what I was before the movement. I remember not as an act of moving back into the past but as a memorial to the struggle of movement. I remember to offer myself the grace to grieve for the person I used to be. In the sentiment of my home community, I may not be where I'm going, but I am grateful that I'm not where I used to be.

FIRST MOVEMENT

Growing up in church, I never really understood Christianity or Jesus. It was never the theology that drew me to church. It was first and foremost the will of my mother who never gave me a choice! Yet, as I remember, I recall that it was something deeper that drew me to church. Like most Black folks now and since slavery, I was drawn to the Black church because it was the only place I felt protected, affirmed, and seen. The Black church was, among many things, a strategy to negotiate the brutality of systematic racism and the unrelenting demands of white supremacist culture to forget centuries of psychophysical trauma. My mom's insistence that I be present was part of how both she and the church loved me. It was and still remains invaluable for the community. It was how I survived. My church upbringing was my first lesson in what a spiritual community was and its power in shaping the lives of all its members.

I rarely agreed with what I was learning, though. I never understood who Jesus was and felt that God was like an old, angry white man. I lived in the South, and old, angry white men were dangerous, so I grew up being afraid of God. On top of that, I slowly began to notice and accept my overwhelming sexual attraction to other men. I barely remember any anti-queer sentiments openly expressed growing up, but what I do remember was the silence that pertained not only to queerness but also to sexuality. The silence was constricting, and it spoke just as loudly as any sermon on the sin of homosexuality. It wasn't until I graduated from high school that I was able to gain distance from the community in order to start articulating my inner experience of my sexuality and body as it related to other male bodies. This particular movement was one of remembering love but privileging the need to speak my own truth.

SECOND MOVEMENT

I ended up attending a small liberal arts college in my hometown that was not very diverse. Because of that and its struggles as a historically white supremacist, heteronormative, queerphobic institution, I would later start referring to the college as a plantation. Though the reference started as a joke born out of my eventual burnout at the school, it was important for me to articulate my experience of the school. The college, much like my later graduate institution, did not actually care about me as a person whose particular intersectionality should be recognized and embraced. The trauma for othered bodies in institutions is the expectation that we should be grateful for being allowed in the door, and, once we are in the door, not much effort is made for us to have a seat at the table. My experience was like being told to sit in the corner and shut up. I call it being a causality of white supremacist grace. Unfortunately, this is not just what many institutions mean by diversity; this is what they mean by inclusivity as well. Despite these criticisms, I came to appreciate my education, relationships with professors and classmates, and the uniqueness of the campus.

However, there were some other experiences. First, after enrolling in a Christian ethics class and finally realizing that I really wasn't a Christian (and according to some of my white evangelical classmates, I was neither ethical nor moral), I knew that I was experiencing a lot of anger toward God. I experienced so much marginalization because of my sexuality and progressive beliefs from people claiming Biblical authority, I dropped the class, scapegoating a lot of rage toward God. In my mind I told him to fuck off and broke up with him. I was no longer interested in being in an abusive relationship. It was perhaps here that the example of Christian practitionership was the hardest for me to reconcile, and I struggled to see the practice as it was demonstrated to me as nothing but psychic violence informed by white supremacy, patriarchy, and class maintenance.

The second experience was 9/11. I was a senior and woke up that day to the feeling of the world falling apart. By the end of the day, I had experienced my first and only anxiety attack as many of my peers were struggling with their own emotional breakdowns. I, like many other people that day, felt a violent jolt. I remember thinking to myself, "People are pushed hard enough to fly planes into skyscrapers! What the fuck!" After that I noticed a significant shift in my community work. Looking back, I actually developed my own personal version of the Four Noble Truths of Buddhism. I understood more intimately that I was suffering, that other people were suffering, that I was a part of other people suffering, and that I was charged with addressing my suffering and the suffering around me. I was understanding that the stakes were incredibly high. That was the beginning of my activism.

The third experience was one that would take years to heal emotionally from. I was new to being an editorial writer for my school paper. I wanted to write a four-part series exposing the obstacles of safer-sex education at the school and began the series with a humorous look at sex and sexuality. That five-hundred-word column changed my life. It ran on Thursday, and by Monday morning of the following week, I had been fired from my on-campus job and became the center of a heated debate over censorship. It triggered perhaps the darkest period of my life. I often tell people that I get how people lose it and conceive of mass shooting and/or suicide. I can't tell you how I made it through a month being openly criticized by students and faculty in public and through the paper. I felt that I had fallen from grace as the "good Negro" and became "that nigger." It was then I began to feel like I was on a plantation. What I learned was the truth of the violence that can come from making white people uncomfortable.

This movement was about survival and experiencing suffering while articulating my truth and learning how to take responsibility for all of it.

THIRD MOVEMENT

I moved to Boston after my graduation. This move was about seeking community to restore the woundedness of my time in college. I sought, above all, to be a member of a community in which my principal struggle was not fighting being othered because of my race, religious beliefs, sexuality, or political views. I moved into an organization called Haley House that was founded in the spirit of the Catholic Worker Movement. It was here that many of my more radical and anarchist social views commingled. It was a time marked by intense devotion to service and activism and living with people dedicated to challenging the systems that create inequality and violence.

And though the community was founded in the tradition of the worker movement, most of my community mates were dharma practitioners or at least meditators. I had taken a world religions class in college in which I found the study of Buddhism interesting, but I felt a stronger pull toward Islam as it was an Abrahamic religion more familiar to my Christian roots. Thus, I did not walk away with an intellectual fascination with dharma. Early during my stay in the community, however, I became very interested in Buddhist philosophy, even meeting some of the teachers my community mates practiced with. I tried meditating but hated it! Still, I was drawn to Buddhism and was surrounded by practitioners. I even took a short break to travel in Asia for the first time, visiting India, and still I did not develop an interest in meditating. It was after my trip to Asia that I no longer had a choice to practice or not.

This movement was about the first calls of dharma.

FOURTH MOVEMENT

I didn't know what clinical depression was until I realized that I was clinically depressed. For me, it was a like demon entering my body and refusing to leave. After my time in Asia, I returned to a sense of heaviness and depleted motivation. Over the course of a few months, my perception of the world devolved into slick grayness. It was hard to make sense of things. I was no longer happy. It was difficult to connect to joy, and when I did, it would always disappear. I couldn't get out of bed, and I spent much of my time alone, isolated in my room listening to Nell Carter sing "Mean to Me" from the Broadway show *Ain't Misbehavin'*. The song is still one of my favorite pieces, but back then it posed a vital question: Why are you so mean to me? I don't know who the *you* was, but I felt oppressed, drained, and numb, like I was dying. The demon was killing me.

One day, I made a vow to myself: I would not die or fade into the grayness. I had been in therapy a few months but didn't find it that helpful and did not have insurance or money to continue treatment. However, my instinct told me to seek guidance from those around me. The community attracted folks of many faith traditions, so I decided to meet with some of them, asking about their paths and what advice they had for me. The meetings were rich, but I was still searching. When a friend recommended that I just start taking medication to manage the illness, I felt a strong and almost violent revolt in my mind. I knew intuitively that if I started meds, I would never be able to get off of them. But I also recognized that I was poised to get much worse with the illness. So I made myself a promise to seek out every possible solution, and when there was nothing left to seek, then medication would be the last resort. These kinds of declarations have a way of opening unexpected doors.

This movement was about learning how to care for my suffering.

FIFTH MOVEMENT

An interesting and fantastic door did open, and I found myself sitting with a Christian healer who promised to help me. I decided to trust this healer. Among the various forms of energy cleansings and aura adjustments, I ended up being taught how to meditate. I had been given meditation instructions before, but now the context was simple and direct: meditate or die. I chose meditation. Along with meditation came a whole lifestyle overhaul, which included nutrition, exercise, limiting the violence I consumed from media, limiting negative folks in my life, and praying to God. By this point in my life I knew that I was at my rock bottom; I was willing to pray to anyone, maybe even the Devil himself! And slowly the healing happened. I was emerging from layers of suffering and darkness, realizing that I had been depressed for longer than I realized, maybe even since high school. As the heaviness lifted, meditation became easier until I had established a daily, simple, open-awareness practice.

My wounding around Christianity was also healing as well. Eventually, I ended my work with the healer and found myself back in the world a new person. I was drawn back into the church and active Bible study. My time in the community had also brought me into a relationship with Christians who modeled their life after Jesus's, and through their example I was finally connecting to Jesus's teachings. I was moved. I was still meditating voraciously. Yet, though I loved being back in church, I was still not a Christian. Theology did not come close to how I deeply felt about reality. I needed teachings that told me the truth about how things really were because part of me wanted to do more than make do, but to ultimately wake up.

This movement was about learning how to move through suffering, finding Jesus, and hearing dharma calling even more clearly.

SIXTH MOVEMENT

When I knew that Dharma was my path, I once again started accompanying my community mates to sittings. This time I was like an open container taking everything in and putting as much as I could into practice. One of the most immediate realizations I experienced was the understanding that dharma communicated how I had felt about the world for as long as I could remember. Dharma revealed the extraordinary complexity of my own experience. Dharma didn't just tell me about love and compassion; it provided a method to become love and compassion. It was through Dharma that I finally understood who Jesus was because I was able to place him within the context of a bodhisattva whose principal motivation is to achieve spiritual awakening to liberate all beings. Most importantly, my formal introduction to karma helped me to see that there is a reason and order behind the way in which things manifest. This understanding helped me take responsibility for my life and helped me to see that the suffering as well as the joy I experienced were related to the choices I had made in previous lives and that the choices I made now would likewise impact what I experienced in the future.

One afternoon, another door opened. I was reading the biography of Ani Tenzin Palmo, *Cave in the Snow*, when three aspirations popped up in my head. They were: 1) I must spend a part of my life in intensive retreat; 2) I must teach others the path of Dharma; and 3) being a Black American with deep concern for social and spiritual issues concerning people of color, I must teach and guide people of color on the path of Dharma in this life. I had never thought of any serious teaching path in Dharma before. I was still a beginner. I hadn't found a teacher, taken refuge or the bodhisattva vow or anything, and here I was having instructions downloaded. It was both extraordinary and mundane at the same time. In the end, I simply said OK.

This movement was about beginning to live dharma out loud!

SEVENTH MOVEMENT

After the download, things moved quickly. I went from being that guy in the back of the meditation hall to entering intensive retreat and teacher training. I knew even then that I was tuning into decisions that had been made before this rebirth. I was just doing what I had been doing for lifetimes before. So much of my life since then has felt like following a script where the plot has already been laid out and my only job is to say my lines. Yet it is more than just saying my lines; it is enacting something that is in concert with my deepest wishes and aspirations.

Eventually, I met my root teacher and found myself in the traditional three-year retreat. My retreat practice provided the opportunity to look at years of pain and woundedness and engage in the struggle of making friends with it and releasing it. It was a time of developing deep love and compassion for myself as I accepted how I had resisted being loved for most of my life. It was also a time of deep forgiveness and learning to trust myself more. There are many ways to describe the experience: silence became the medium in which I was reborn into a sense of happiness and contentment. But overall, it ushered me into a period of thriving and flourishing in my life. After completing the retreat, I was authorized as a lama in the Kagyu School of Tibetan Buddhism.

This last and current movement has been about entering into a golden age in my life. This age is not free of suffering, but it is full of love and happiness that embrace my suffering. I am not the person I used to be. I have journeyed over many miles and tears to be able to share this story. In the end my movements have cost me. They have cost me my fear of becoming the person that I want and need to be. I write this only because I needed to read something like this when I was most lost in my wandering and aching.

In the words of Sweet Honey in the Rock, "We're almost home." One day, may all beings find their homeland after the great wandering.

THE ABOLITION OF WHITENESS

by Jasmine Syedullah, PhD

I've lived in predominantly white spaces my whole life. Though it wasn't ever easy, I was about twenty or so before I began to experience the ubiquity of whiteness as a real problem. By the time I entered my first predominantly white private school in Brooklyn I was already primed for the immersion. As a young person in the Midwest, I could not escape the everyday supremacy of whiteness. It saturated my Saturday morning television shows, my young adult reading practices. It followed me to school and found me in dreams.

I learned to appear unflappable under pressure, and I could bear a lot. I made friends, paid attention, followed instructions, and was generally rewarded for being articulate, bright, curious, but conflict adverse. My time was split between home and church. My family home was itself the property of the church, the rectory of the parish of which my father was priest. The places we called home were owned by others, by institutions. The impositions of whiteness became an existential crisis. I had to unseat myself from the hearth of whiteness and find another place to call home.

I began to sit in college, which was the "lab" assignment of a religious studies course on theories and practices of Buddhism I found my junior year. I was looking for a major, but what I found beneath the veil of the good student, the model minority, the happy sidekick, was someone else and she was screaming. I could not bear to hear her at all until I arrived at my cushion. There was nothing special about that morning except that I recall the room feeling especially still. After a few moments my breathing exercises fell away and the racing thoughts ran out of fuel. There was just the feeling of breathing, following my breath as it filled my body, gently rising and cresting like waves through the pores of my skin. Then I felt it. It was not bliss; it was not nirvana. It started in my stomach, a violent kind of grief-like pain—the slow eruption of shattered glass began to rise like a volcano up from my core like so much indigestible garbage. I did not dare move. I did not yet know what I was feeling. I would only put words to it later. It was a blinding rage. It was a bottomless sadness. I had been at home in whiteness so long I had no idea how abandoned I felt in my own body. I kept breathing. I did not want to run from it, from myself. This feeling was a part of me that had been there a long time, but I'd been failing to pay attention. Later I would wonder how I had managed to keep all that inside without feeling it, to stay so distracted from myself I could not even hear myself screaming. For days afterward I walked around campus like my best friend had betrayed me. She had. I could not trust myself. I found myself a stranger.

Though I did not know it yet, this was the first leg of my escape from whiteness. One of the things that had drawn me to Buddhism was the notion of no self. I was fascinated by the prospect of being Jasmine and not being Jasmine. I did not realize that before I could decenter myself, there had to be a self to decenter. I would have to discover who I was beneath all that self-hatred. It did not feel like transcendence. It felt more like heartbreak. Racism was not the only thing curdling my insides. It was all the things—I was not becoming what my world expected me to be, and it was not something I was supposed to fix or overcome. It was something I would have to sit with. So I did. Even though it brought me to tears, I kept sitting—at first because my semester grade counted on it, but then because sitting informally with friends on the campus green or in the chapel or by myself in my room was waking something up. A sadness. A loneliness I did not understand but did not want to go away. I was learning to tell the truth about myself. To stand up for her instead of run away. I was mining the painful ruins of my efforts to overcome this tokenized exceptionalism, the precarity of model minority meritocracy. I had been struggling to pass—not with my skin because, as the darkest in my family, looking white was far from fathomable— but by acting like my Blackness didn't really matter. I had been unwittingly passing off rage as charm, and I had no clue how to stop. Who to tell?

My rage became this strange new companion that I had no idea how to integrate with the total eclipse of my own happily assimilated performance of self. After I tried to talk to my parents, I tried to talk to my friends. Most of them were white. My boyfriend was white. My first heartbreak was a white woman. All but two of my professors, all but one of my teaching assistants. I was picking fights with my roommates. I resented their gait, their cadence, the casual gestures with which they signified entitlement, with which they moved the world. I did not love sitting, but I did it because it was giving me space to see myself more clearly. I was starting to see all the ways I write myself off, lock myself out, or straight-up shut myself down. I could see how I was not acting alone. Many of the people, places, and activities I invested in reinforced my self-erasure. I needed to go.

I moved from Providence to San Francisco in the summer of 2002. I got a part-time job at a drop-in center at the YMCA in the Tenderloin. There was a large floor-to-ceiling window in the game room that looked out onto the streets of San Francisco. Outside the window, lines of houseless folks lined the block at least once a week to receive life-saving AIDS/HIV drugs. Outside the window police body-tackled Black and brown brothers to the ground and forcibly probed their privacy on the concrete for contraband. I wrote poetry. I found family in a hip-hop guerrilla-theater, spoken-word, sketch activism-performance troupe. I found family with the founders of *POOR Magazine*, led by the dear poverty scholar and spiritual guide Dee and her daughter Tiny on Sixth and Market. I found myself at the all-girl dive bar on Lexington and Nineteenth. There were many new outlets for the screaming. They were not all safe, but they were far healthier than snuffing out my light in a veil of silence. The problem with being at home in whiteness is that it goes hand-in-glove with the presumption that everything whiteness does must be best, right, noble, beautiful, moral, and productive. The problem with becoming myself was that, no matter how nice I had learned to be, no matter how smart or accommodating, sitting with myself meant I was becoming more myself, more Black. As soon as I started getting good at being human I was increasingly perceived as a threat.

Dharma practice called my attention to the deepest of my investments in white supremacy and made me feel, without sugar coats, without apology or redemption, how deeply destructive it is to live in the afterlife of slavery as the embodied and constant reminder of the unexamined trauma of the white experience. Homeleaving began on the cushion, as a sometime mediation pastime curated by a tenured professor at an Ivy League school. It became a practice when I met my dharma teacher. She is an angel in the form of a dragon. Her dharma was not all Namaste Namaste. Her practice was fiery, full-on gangster compassion, unapologetically Black. It queered the calm of the sitting sensibility I had seen elsewhere, and it was not a practice afraid of sound, of sorrow or song, of people catching the spirit and making joyful noises even in the stillness of the *zendo*. Rev. angel's practice evolved a lot over the years I sat with her, but the feeling of belonging in a deep sense was always there—welcoming my Blackness.

I had been to many practice centers—Zen, Vipassana. I was turned off to nearly every single one and almost never returned after the first visit. When I walked through the door, I saw no one like me there. It did not matter how nice folks were. With no one of color, at least no one relatable, I felt like I needed to maintain that appearance of self-sufficiency I had picked up in school, being both good and unflappable. I did not want to have to be charming to belong. I could not be in one more place where my fury or grief or truth of my feelings of isolation might be misread or become an imposition. I needed the people around me holding my practice to get that more than I did.

By the time I met Rev. angel, my anger had developed a voice but not a center. I was not quite out of control, but lack of an ability to center meant I was reactionary, compulsive. I was learning to pay attention to myself, to my feelings, but they felt uncontainable, like they were consuming me. Rev. angel was a beacon in a storm I felt too capsized to reach. But I kept swimming. We met at a Black Health Summit in Oakland, and I recall feeling both enchanted by her presence and her voice and combative with her insistence that, if you don't know what to do, just keep sitting. *Well, I already know that*, I thought to myself. "What if you don't like what all you find there?" I asked. "Just keep sitting," she said. I was not satisfied, but I was not ready to walk away either. It took a few months for me to let that land. When I took the leap and biked the whole ten blocks to her Center, located at that time on the border of North Oakland and South Berkeley, I went because, despite the fact that I felt like she did not answer my question, I still felt scattered, easily overstretched, overwhelmed, and distracted. I had the feeling that I might finally be finding my way toward myself by biking to her practice hall—that I might have found in a teacher someone who might be able to hear me scream. I could sit with her. Screaming inside. And it would be OK.

She, along with the incredible crew, the *sangha* I found there—ringing bells, sweeping floors, arranging flowers, making dinner—never policed how I showed up. They were just genuinely happy that I did, even when there were lapses. Even if I didn't call. There was no pretense. I was not their token. Rev. angel would actually call out whatever felt funky as soon as it arose, and we faced it as a group. She wouldn't let me disappear into myself. She would name it, if she saw me trying to be at home in whiteness, exceptionalism, mammie mentality, and would have no qualms asking me to stop, adjust my posture, and take up the room I occupy and no more. *Mind your business* is one of her favorite teachings. I needed someone to give me permission to leave pretense and find home in myself, in my own power before I could decenter my ego. I needed directions about how to keep going in the face of institutional racism, sexism, and homophobia. I needed someone strong enough to hold the space of my practice without being nice, with no apologies for the way she expressed her love. I needed a *sangha* led by fierce-ass emotionally expressive passionate queer women of color. I needed to be surrounded by role models/practitioners who were, like me, extraordinary and perfectly imperfect.

We were waking up together, with and against the grain of each other's practice, and it could get messy. The harder it got to stay, the more we learned to reflect to each other the costs of the other's attachments to perfection, to exceptionalism, to status. We could be angry in the service to our liberation, and even when it didn't "work," it was a blessing. It was a blessing to be practicing with people who were invested in falling out of love with innocence, invisibility, and compartmentalization. As practitioners within a variation on the theme of Zen, nobility, beauty, morality, and efficiency were integral. It was inevitable that our most deft expressions of them could also lack integrity, cause injury, and perpetuate harm. The point wasn't to try to be utterly extraordinary, it was that the utterly extraordinary also made mistakes.

The tiptoeing around race and other forms of difference as if in fear of waking a sleeping lion is one of the most subtly toxic attributes of whiteness in our culture right now. Everyone fears making mistakes. For white folks, though, the coexistence of being historically lauded as the creators of what is right, making mistakes must be hard. We are all waking up. It is going to get messy. The good news is there are brooms, and there are rags. Domestic labor has long fallen from a place of culturally respected work—something about it being the badge of submission for many thousands gone, bodies stolen, forcibly extracted from homelands, and scattered throughout the globe to modernize the new world. The practice of sitting required me to abolish the supremacy of whiteness that lived in myself and make a practice of doing so on the regular, with every breath so the volcanic pressure, the grief, and rage have witness and release without boiling up and exploding all over my newly found sense of self.

From the cushion to the teacher to the *sangha* there was not a lack, an insufficiency to be overcome, an imperfection to be corrected. I just needed to be loved and learn to love myself not because of what I could do, or how well I could do it, but just because I showed up on this planet and deserve to feel like it wasn't a bad idea for me to be here. *Sangha* is a Sanskrit word meaning association, assembly, company, or community. *Sangha* taught me that homeleaving means letting go of the desire to save master from himself. It means learning to let people go, and to even let them go back home. *Sangha* has taught me to mind the gap between what we say and what we do. The practice pulls us together, but we are not all headed in the same direction at the same time. We long for community but do not know how to sit with difference. We try to take connection and eviscerate what makes us distinct. Just as the commuter watches for the train from the busy platform, I have watched the crowds try to form community, peeling into the station, pooling together, waiting on the arrival of their most trusted form of transportation. Time passes, and we grow anxious. So many promises. Such promising destinations. We can get lost in all the excitement of waiting for deliverance from the presence of what bell hooks so wisely names *white supremacist capitalist patriarchy*. We can get so obsessed in the anticipation of reaching a sense of escape, of touching this shiny, intoxicating promise that when the train arrives, we don't think. We jump on board! Won't any way out of isolation do? Maybe if we all just board the next one, we can get there all at once. We might all shuttle ourselves onto the train and just as the doors close we hear the station announcer call out, "Come on! Whiteness is waiting!" *But, wait,* we think. *Wasn't this supposed to be the train to awakening, away from whiteness?* We misread the signs again and again.

So we get off at the next station. We sit and practice staying on the platform. We find ourselves practicing everywhere. On the cushion. On the train. With the *sangha*. Off the path. On the way. Everywhere whiteness appears to be the golden ticket. The short cut. The glory of the few. The chosen. The entitled. The justification for injury. The use of force. The state of the exceptional. We wonder how whiteness could be both the problem and the best exit strategy. The problem and the final solution.

I've mistakenly stumbled back homebound on the bullet train time and time again. Though I am sure I will find myself there again, after years and years of being home in the exception, in the aggravated assault of its domestic violence, I am no longer enjoying the ride. I am just sick and bored. Bored to death and frustrated with this habituation toward the supremacy of whiteness. We've been in this station for a long time. It is clear now. There is no train other than those that take us backward. There is no deliverance. We are not going anywhere. It's time to stop waiting. It is time to connect some other way, turn to each other, turn the station into a new homestead and find new ways to imagine progress, practice new protocols of connection. What began as individual acts of rebellion, desires to be exceptional, can become a collective opportunity for a reorientation of our shared fugitivity. Whiteness is not the frontier. It is not an adventure. It's a road to nowhere. It's a captivity narrative. And there is another way out of its domain. Just keep sitting, she said.

A DIFFERENT DRUM

by Rev. angel Kyodo williams, Sensei

EVERYTHING BEGINS BY LEAVING

People always ask about beginnings. We strive after newness, the shiny, the acquisition of possibility. A proxy for our own longing to begin anew on the journey of finding ourselves because we haven't yet gotten there. What we don't often ask is, "What made me choose me?" and "What had to end?" and "What got left behind?"

STAGES AND VOWS

Perhaps it had just come out, I don't remember any longer, but the bright yellow cover of M. Scott Peck's book *The Different Drum* caught my eye's attention, though it was its title that caught my soul. I had always been a different drum, even when I looked the same. Most of my early life was spent desperately wanting to be the same, trying to fit the molds handed to me and the ones I thought I belonged in, only to realize with stunning certainty that I, in fact, did not. Rinse. Wash. Repeat.

Peck's proposed stages eventually provided a lens through which I continue to envision the spiritual and the political life journeys as simultaneously parallel and intertwined. More acutely, Peck's stages gave me the answer to a question I'd held in stubborn arrogance, one that prevented me from seeing people who counted themselves part of some religion—most especially Christianity—with respect. By that time, I had developed growing admiration for obvious figures like Desmond Tutu, His Holiness the Dalai Lama, but also Malcolm X and the great Dalit hero and liberator of the Untouchables, Bhimrao Ambedkar. They were, by all appearances, religious. But they seemed smart, reasonable, and deeply concerned with social justice, too. Not only did Peck's description of development unseat the stubborn aversion I had to other people's religiosity, it also freed me to accept my own path as not just philosophical but spiritual, too.

It becomes clear on any journey into one's truth that homeleaving happens more than once in our lives, and from many different places we once considered home. Turns out that the Four Vows, written for ordinary lay folk as far back as 1,500 years ago, and uttered at the end of every Zen practice session, speak to each of Peck's stages. I take these vows again and again, marking my life's journey through these stages as practice. I envision my first homeleaving through both the stages and vows here:

STAGE I: CHAOS–EARLY CHILDHOOD: TOLD WHERE TO GO, WILLED AND CONTROLLED

Beings are numberless; I vow to save them all.

Like many children born "into" a religion or tradition, Christianity by way of the Black Baptist Church wasn't a choice I was given so much as a place I was made to go. I was toted along like a shiny Sunday handbag. It meant having my hair pulled and twisted into pristine "Shirley Temple curls," spotless white patent leather shoes with pom-pom socks sitting just so beneath unscuffed caramel brown knees, dresses of just enough delicate white lace and frills so that there was never a safe place to sit, and a paper doily pinned uncomfortably to my head.

My earliest recollection of a life utterly controlled by an abusive babysitter-turned-pseudo-mom was the weekly pomp and circumstance of going to church. It is also the most poignant reminder of the gross conflict between the life we lived in full view of everyone and the one that went down behind closed doors where the yelling, shaming, emotional manipulation, arm-twisting, head-thrust-into-the-flushing-toilet scenes were performed alongside the rehearsal of stories that obscured the truth.

My father was raised Catholic. D took care of me from soon after my mother left to spare herself my father's philandering. He was a firefighter by night and day, and a womanizer in the spaces between. It was the early '70s—love was free and boys will be boys, after all. D was seventeen when she came into my life. She used to live around the corner in a chaotic house teeming with a rotating cast of foster children, along with a few long-termers who became siblings in name. From the beloved blond, blue-eyed but clearly mixed John-John to the taunted, dark, mentally challenged—we used "retarded" back then— Tracy Boy and barely remembered Tracy Girl, D's imposing Big Momma Church Lady Mrs. Robinson cast a watchful eye over them all. The collecting of disparate, desperate children must've had a long history because D's sister Heather was the same age, white as they come, but loud, brash, and ghetto. D was herself red-bone bright with gleaming hazel eyes and a big, welcoming smile. No one would suspect she was a faithful product of the good and pious church lady's den of abuse and molestation that was held together by fear.

It was D's church I first recall. I liked the choir, so I tried to make it work, but it never really did—the other big church ladies fanning, folks faintin' and hollerin' as they caught the Holy Ghost streaking down the aisles. The pretense of Sunday-only proper manners in other peoples' company mixed with stylized high drama fit for its own reality show and threw into relief the falsehood of my own overwhelming existence.

My role was to submit to the highest and most fearful authority, and I did as I was willed. My lighter skin and springy "good hair" that could be tightly controlled made me the best kind of windup doll. A child model who was a model child: starting school early but still commanding the three Rs better than anyone, being brilliant in every way as if by shining so bright no one would really see me and the suffering I endured.

STAGE II: FORMAL—ADHERENCE TO ORDER AND RULES

Desires are inexhaustible; I vow to put an end to them.

By the time I was eight, D's sadistic ways had been found out. Both the harrowed life and only motherly love I could remember disappeared overnight.

My father's relationship with his newest girlfriend was serious enough to take us to Brooklyn. It was the heart of Flatbush and the height of the West Indian population explosion there. I was a foreigner in my own homeland, navigating a sea of Black faces that I felt neither kin nor camaraderie with. The golden years of living in the wildly multicultural Lefrak City—a kind of United Nations of massive housing in Queens—were now behind me. The safety of being different among difference was left against my will. The Brooklyn years were spent in hiding.

With my newly dubbed stepmother and her daughter, my stepsister, who were fair-skinned—much "yellower" than I, as was common for lighter Jamaicans—a vague sense of superiority wafted in the air. "High and mighty" they were. And I was different from them because I wasn't as new to the country and was in fact a Yankee to boot. Many of the West Indians despised us Yankees for our mis-storied laziness, and yet envied the security of citizenship; we were all caught in the territorial wars waged between Black bodies vying for a higher place on the lowest rung of the totem pole reserved for us in the land of the freely white. The Hasidic Jews and Italians eventually receded to the higher ground that white-skinned people always seem to find when a tide of Black and brown rolls in. Rather than seeing ourselves as aligned, we were repositioned as bottom-feeders fighting among ourselves for the rotting remnants and decay white folks left behind.

I passed the years becoming invisible behind comic books walking to and from school, slinking in the hallways to avoid the loud, sharp-tongued children. They found my combination of the proper English my father insisted on, lighter skin, longish hair—unruly but with natural curls—sharp mind, and wide-eyed naiveté too tempting an island to let exist uninvaded. "Ya t'ink ya white, gerl?"

When intelligence is what bought you some relief, at least among the adults, it became the cards you played, holding them close when the stakes were too high and bluffing to make your way through.

My stepmother had an enormous white King James–version of the Bible gilded in gold. Along with the twenty-one-book set of brown and Black World Book Encyclopedias and Child-craft books she sold and I immersed myself in, that Bible became yet another hiding place for me, much like my art teacher Mr. Goldstein's tiny storage room office that I evaded the entire sixth grade in. My new stepmother's Episcopalian church was a welcome relief from the ecstatic drama of D's church. I took refuge not so much in the church but in the silence I found.

While I was always skeptical, the stories were entertaining enough, so I perused the Bible. Dissecting the scenarios provided hours of fodder for my imagination: the greatest refuge of the shy, introverted, non-belonging. I secretly wanted to be a priest but was already a "tomboy" and knew women in the church and military had to wear dresses, which wasn't happening now that I had a say.

Me and Jesus were getting along fine. I knew things didn't turn out the best for Christ given the images of the emaciated and wounded white man with pained blue eyes I'd grown up with, but I wasn't prepared for confronting his agony.

About the ninth hour, Jesus cried out with a loud voice, saying, "Eli, eli, lama sabachthani"—My God, my God, why hast thou forsaken me?—Matthew 27:45 and 46

I was angry. How could God forsake him? What kind of good could this God ever be if so cruel? He'd turned his back while his only child suffered alone and in the dark. For some time, I imagined my anger was because I couldn't make sense of it, but really, I couldn't make sense of how I had been left to bear a burden so great so young because the people in my life—my own father, too—had forsaken me.

STAGE III: DOUBT–SKEPTICISM, REJECTION OF RULES AS GIVEN, INDIVIDUAL INVESTIGATION

The truth is boundless; I vow to perceive it.

By age twelve, I'd excused myself from Sunday school, church, and eventually Christianity. School provided me with science as a less painful story of human existence, and my time devouring World Book Encyclopedias gave me access to agnosticism. I was already savvy enough to calculate the risk of being atheist should my scientific lean be proven wrong, so I opted for the less certain path of disowning the cruel God with indifference, rather than suggest he didn't exist at all.

Along with a fascination for the logical orderliness of science came a disdain for the obvious absurdity of the childish stories of the Bible … and the people who believed them.

'Tweens and Twenties

Mercifully, I escaped Brooklyn and went to live with my mother in lower Manhattan, though I straddled the Brooklyn Bridge and the vastly different worlds it joined together more often than not. The harshness and violence of Flatbush was tempered by the Bohemian understated class of Tribeca. Both of them were set against the backdrop of a Chinatown school that was more than mostly ethnic Chinese, so I lived again as a foreigner in familiar land. I learned that context was everything, dictating norms of culture, speech, expression of gender, intelligence, and the rules for how to belong. This bridging, as both survival function and choiceful act, taught me a basic Truth: Each world you inhabit is no more or less real than the others. It is all just a protocol, a made-up and agreed-upon set of codes. In fact, moving fluidly between worlds of difference meant developing an awareness of what of "so-called you" remained still and apparently the same.

In my high school years, I explored the wide-open land of no real parental oversight. Cutting school. Lounging in the upscale diner in Chelsea learning the cheeky talk and refinement of everything from gay white men. They came in stronger and stronger waves, with their dinner parties, studs, and leather boys, washing over the mostly Puerto Rican and Black families that lived there until those families were drowning and almost none.

Rolling up in lesbian, then gay, then mixed clubs through the night, I reveled in the last deep breaths of queer culture in the West Village in the '80s. We didn't know it was dying then because *we* felt most alive when we were taking over the west strip of Washington Square Park all the way down Christopher Street to the span on the Hudson it met, simply known as The Pier. We had a place to be out on the streets, proud to be ourselves. We tested the boundaries of our boldness and practiced holding hands, kissing, loving, fighting, and fucking where everyone could see. Defiantly doing out loud what straight people took for granted, we were finding and freeing ourselves in the one place we could. It wasn't always safe, but it was ours, and communities formed by truth mattered more than delusions of safety. A natural aversion to the disorderliness of drugs and my high-minded downtown disgust with the sloppiness of being drunk kept me relatively safe in those days.

Meanwhile, Madonna took *vogueing* from our nighttime runways and onto the mainstream stage. It wasn't long before the runways rolled up behind her with Paris Burning as AIDS thinned our numbers and dampened the glee of our balls-out freedom. In the meantime—maybe in response?—gender was becoming more complex. You were no longer policed into a strictly female or male role-play inside of being Lesbian or Gay. BT and eventually Q were finding their way into our landscape and language. We were finding new allies, paving new intersections, telling new stories and seeding a Queer Nation by reclaiming what was meant to shame us. It felt radical and emergent. I was alive and fighting for justice. And then I had to leave.

A trip to San Francisco landed me on a cushion in the temple made famous in my mind by reading Shunryu Suzuki Roshi's book *Zen Mind, Beginner's Mind*. I'd found it by accident rummaging through New York's old Tower Books. The chance to try out meditation beyond my closeted setup at home was too much to pass up, even if I had to make my way through an unknown city, already farther away from home than I'd ever been. More than leaving home and my sleeping lover, I'd begun to leave my former self in the still shadowy dawn light that September morning.

I was in my first adult relationship, had found my activist voice, and was thinking seriously about my life and where it was going. My partner's wealth made me aware of class. Everything else made me aware of the limitation assumed for colored girls to transcend class, or anything else for that matter. So I carved out a comfortable space in my identity as colored, female, and queer. I decided, as was being suggested in my new Zen practice, to enter it completely.

By now I had managed to navigate my way up, having sacrificed my Christmas break for my first weeklong Zen retreat to walk in circles staring at a gaggle of white peoples' feet. I knew I had left the performance of hip somewhere on the café-turned-dance-floor under the dimmed lights.

Not too much longer after, I knowingly carried my tender grief to the funeral of my relationship with my now grown-up friends. The truth I was seeking was more and more at odds with the stories we told ourselves to be right, to keep fear and overwhelming at bay. Standing increasingly on the outside and no longer wanting to be in, I turned and walked away, leaving my friends behind.

STAGE IV: MYSTIC/COMMUNAL

Liberation is unattainable; I vow to attain it.

The intersections and influencers of my life left little room for some outside and some in.

Black, white, mixed, Cherokee, Blackfoot. High yellow and sweet berry Black. The Catholic that never was. The Baptist, agnostic heathen, not Buddhist but Zen priest. Poster child modeling pain, foreigner in my own land. Being in the territory doesn't make you belong. Every time I tried to stay within the lines, they ran over me, so I chose the borderlands and left divisions behind.

The hero and liar that nurtured me. The mother-punisher who stole from me and stole for me, raised me up and shoved me down. The church lady dealing sin dressed as saint, building a house of protection and pain. The fierce queens from the runways who sex-danced their way to early deaths and lived forever on screen. The Black and brown boys gone to prison, queer colored girls behind bars and behind sassiness that reminded me where I might have been. Chelsea fags and muscle boys with the manners and motivation to leave. The low-key, high-brow urban Bohemians who showed me How to Sit with the invisible cloak of class on, a formless field of benefaction, to exude the quiet cool my Zen would one day be.

Whenever I feel around for me, I find all of them and someone else I didn't know was there before. I want for their liberation because, inside theirs, I found mine. The dharma that I would come to taught me everything I already knew about life—that it is indeed suffering, and the path of liberation is paved with pain and joy but always near when you know you're just looking to return to you and have to leave the home of Me behind.

Enter here. It's everywhere and in everyone.

SECTION II:

STAKEHOLDERS—WHAT WE BRING FORWARD

BRINGING OUR WHOLE SELVES:
A THEORY OF QUEER DHARMA

Radical Dharma emerges from a lineage of insurgence that is about bringing our whole selves. We can't marginalize others or ourselves as part of our pursuit of liberation, personal or political. We couldn't have arrived here without a fuller and fuller fullness. The leaders of antiracist movements have always included people of many sexual and gender orientations. Throughout our conversations, the deep connection between personal liberation and social transformation is increasingly clear. It is embodied. In the following, we share testimonies and dialogue on the dharma of sexuality and gender identity and how they have been a part of our own practices of personal liberation.

TESTIMONIES: QUEER IS AS QUEER DOES

TESTIMONY I: JASMINE

I was six years old when I decided I was a unicorn. Recess was canceled that day because it was raining. We all sat on the floor in the dark as a rain storm pounded the roof of our kindergarten classroom. On the TV/VCR they played a movie about a restless unicorn who, though she was happy, found herself alone—the last of her kind. My six-year-old self identified with her isolation and trembled at the moment she had to leave the safety of her forest to begin her journey to find and eventually free others like her held captive somewhere far away. Those who saw her for who she was could see her power was immeasurable, a thing of hope and healing, but to most she appeared a thing to be hunted, domesticated, traded, and controlled—dispossessed of the ability to wander far. Her journey to free the others required her transformation. It wasn't a strategy she chose, but rather one that chose her. While she did not change willingly, in order to survive she had to accept the new forms she found herself inhabiting. Watching that movie in the same classroom where earlier that year I'd been reprimanded and forcibly punished for the flirtatious act of competitively flashing another Black girl on the playground weeks before (show me yours and I'll show you mine!) somehow clued me in, if only subconsciously, to the kinds of transformation my own coming into being queer might require should I attempt to embrace my new form, desire, damage, doubt, and all.

I could not embrace it all at once. Over time, almost by accident, desire began to displace my fear of my freedom. Far before I learned to theorize it, liberation leaped up out of ordinary moments and shook loose the shy, shamed, and shaking trappings of useless labels, conventions, and identities. Dancing became a way to actively disorient my relationship to myself, my sexuality, my story about my desire. I was not looking for liberation when transformation chose me. I was looking for the others and found myself becoming queer—what started as an innocent mistake began to feel like magic. Desire could not stay static. I chose to let its propensity for transformation choose me, leaving space for mere feeling to jump the rules of time and become for an instant immortal. It was not pretty, or kind, or convenient. It was honest and healing and humbling. I wanted to learn the art of liberation in a book, or on a cushion—in the isolation of my self-reliance rather than in the messy company of others. But the ethics of desire could not be attained in the absence of the pressure proximity so queerly produced. Alhamdulillah!

TESTIMONY II: LAMA ROD

When I say queer, I am remembering the first time another man touched me, how my body convulsed, being consumed by its own appetite. Or remembering *Giovanni's Room* and wondering if another man would ever crave me like Giovanni craved David, wondering if James Baldwin was born only to sing to me. Or like remembering falling in love with other boys, knowing that even if that love was never returned, it was so much more than never knowing how to love at all. Or remembering as I grew older, learning the potential of love beyond gender or sex. Or remembering when Audre Lorde said *the erotic* to the mothers and daughters, how she at the same time ransomed my body out of lands of men yoking me to simple gifts between their legs.

Then remembering Essex Hemphill whispering how I could be a revolution without bloodshed. And remembering coming out, saying the words, opening the door that I could never close again. Saying my secret name to the world, bringing my loving, aching, and craving for other bodies and minds like mine into language, and how the world noticed me for the first time, curtsied, but then greeted me in a friendship that often felt like acts of psychic and physical violence. Or remembering meeting the Dharma and how it held the trauma of my struggle to love through my sexuality warmly and kindly, how compassion meant realizing that I was not the only battered one in the world. Or remembering when I surrendered to my love of radical thought and action, knowing that queerness, radicalism, and Dharma were all acts of remembering myself as the *beloved* wanting to be free in the world and that it would be by my will and hands that the world would become home. It is remembering me, saying my own name, wanting me at the end of the day. This is what I mean by queer.

TESTIMONY III: REV. ANGEL

Queerness paved the way for my entering the dharma. Rather than trying to colonize, commodify, or compartmentalize it, I could let it enter me. I could let painful truths that had been hidden away emerge on my cushion because through choosing queerness I had already had practice *choosing* to be free. I knew that it meant allowing myself to be seen and that fully accepting myself is an inherently binding agreement of allowing others to be fully themselves.

Letting my bisexual lovers be who they are rather than insisting that they choose was a practice of queer radical dharma because it meant finding where I was threatened by a sense of inferiority when stacked against men and the potential loss of love that raised. When I realized that queerness couldn't be limited to sex and sexuality, that to choose queer expressed something more profound about who and how we are, I had to shift my worldview to one that sees beyond binary truths handed to us to yoke ourselves into a system of control. To hold queerness as a practice is to be in active radical acceptance of everyone and all things as they are.

DESIRE AND THE DHARMA

FEMALE SPEAKER: I've been practicing Buddhism for a couple years now. Sometimes I get conflicted by the traditional ways of thinking: Can you be sexually liberated and still be a Buddhist? I feel as if sometimes it's shunned, like taking our bodies as desire. What is it about dharma and sexuality that connects and why? How would you describe the complementary of dharma, minority sexuality, and minority race in the U.S.? Thank you.

JASMINE: Yes! I was really struck in reading all of our testimonies at how irreverently sensual they were; I was really enjoying that. It is not something that I associate with sitting on a cushion.

REV. ANGEL: Fundamentally one of the questions at the seat of Dharma is desire. So it is very interesting that desire, in terms of sexuality, is rather seldomly spoken about. Everyone is navigating desire as part of their practice. I think it is a fundamental aspect of being human. People who are claiming heterosexuality have the privilege to leave that conversation aside, though. They have the privilege of leaving the conversation about their desire and what is going on with them sexually outside of their practice. They don't have to present themselves through a conversation about their sexuality in the way queer people tend to as a way of being seen and known. People who are queer do not have the privilege of not naming or claiming their queerness on the path to being whole.

LAMA ROD: We have been traditionally silent around the expression of sexuality. When I came into Dharma, one of the first things that I had to work with was how I was taught to relate to my own body and thoughts on sexuality. I started breaking through into this tremendous woundedness that I had been denying. This was the radical piece, but for me the queerness and radicalism and Dharma really started to feed into one another. So Dharma is queerness, and queerness is Dharma to me and all that is radical. Dharma is essentially the training to be free just as radical and queerness is the training to be free. My identification with queer is very conscious because I was put on the spot and felt that I couldn't make different choices. As a gay man I had really narrowly defined kinds of attractions. So identifying with queer has kind of opened the space up completely even though it was social, political. It was just the space I needed to explore transgression in a way that I couldn't when I only identified as a gay man.

I wanted to love beyond attachment or fixation to certain kinds of bodies. James Baldwin came along and actually reading his words, I realized that being gay was much more than the sex, it was about intimate connection to other men. It was very difficult for me to experience because I was struggling to develop a relationship with my own body to feel good. Great sex was fun, but there was more that I wanted. It is a bit difficult for me to articulate, but as I get older it is about connecting to people and finding that connection to be attractive, just that basic connection that is beginning to transcend sex and gender. Within attraction, sexual desire is part of the experience but not the totality of the experience for me. I had to begin to make that choice to transcend the basic appetite and desire for body where I find myself being at odds with other gay men. It is about liberation. It is about awareness and about an understanding of who and what we are. It is important for me to honor the teachers that I had before the Buddha and before the Dharma came along. James Baldwin was my teacher;

Audre Lorde was my teacher. Essex Hemphill was my teacher. These are the writers that first helped me to eventually find the Dharma through leaning into myself as a sexual being, and these are the teachers that helped me love my sexuality and my sexual expression.

REV. ANGEL: I was invited to sit with a circle of white folks that were teachers and administrative leaders of a sprawling Buddhist community in the region. One of the questions they asked was, "What do you see?" I have the unique privilege of visiting different traditions and lineages. I get to take a bird's eye view.

Queer people of color appear to be the fastest growing demographic entering into Buddhist communities. I find that striking. I'm sure that's not true everywhere, but if I mix the whole thing together, from what I hear rumbling on the ground, that seems to be reasonably true, and it makes complete sense to me.

There is an article that was written years ago by Dr. Christopher Queen. He talks about B. R. Ambedkar, who was Gandhi's contemporary, who was born Untouchable. For all intents and purposes, he's a Black man in terms of his caste and his rank and society, and there's a whole side story about his challenge and push back against Gandhi. But he ultimately came to the conclusion that Untouchability was fixed within the Hindu religion. So he would find another religion, and he did a great deal of study.

He was the writer of the [Indian] constitution, so he was very intelligent and well-educated and bright. He had to really work at this effort of studying world religions and, strangely enough, he ended back in [the] religion that originated in his own homeland: Buddhism. The reason he ended up there was because the teachings expressed the most openness to accepting anyone as they are. So it's embedded in the teaching and the feeling space of Buddhism to be spacious and allowing of who you are as you are. That has been since obstructed by human intervention and foible. But I think that's what we're seeing. Difference fits.

LAMA ROD: In my tradition, I've felt a lot of freedom to enter and reimagine a self that was very liberatory. There was this space where queerness wasn't so important, but rather it was the intention of my life and how I used these identities to help people and to help myself. I was being really taught that attachment to identity is another way in which we are fixated on this sense of self. I was taught a lot of space around queerness that was deeply healing for me. Tibetan Buddhism was made for queer people. The pretty colors, the iconography, the deities are really gender queer. I mean, you can't figure out the gender of these deities. Look at a *thangka*. Men wear dresses. There's pageantry and ritual. It's like a parade. [Laughter]

REV. ANGEL: I'm going to have to interrupt because that was the opposite for me. Zen was the only thing that was going to get me in a dress. [Laughter] And we had gender-neutral terms, so I got to be a priest, not a priestess. This is in contrast to the messages that many of us received if we grew up in Christianity. There are so many explicit messages against being queer or even expressing sexuality.

LAMA ROD: I think we have more questions. But there's no affirmative action in our tradition. I wasn't accepted into training because I was Black. Even though I am one of the first Black lamas in my lineage. And with my teacher I had to do everything that everyone else did: I had to learn Tibetan. I had to do 100,000 prostrations. I had to sit in the box for three years. I had to hold vows. And people don't get that. They see me, they think, "Oh, you're cool." [Laughter]

We have to interrogate this body shame, this sex shame that we're born into. And we have to learn how to liberate ourselves even from that. How [do] we practice sexuality with the changes that we're making? Are we allowing people to make the changes they need to make to be happy, to do what feels good but which doesn't hurt themselves or other people around them?

GET WHAT YOU NEED

LAMA ROD: The *sangha* is very important because it can reflect the things that we're missing, that we're bypassing.

When I talk about *sangha*, I talk about it as the space where we're rubbing against each other and we're coming into contact and there's conflict. This conflict isn't normal conflict, it isn't worldly conflict, because when we enter into sacred community, we have a different obligation. We see our interactions as pointing us back to things we need to look at more closely. We're being reminded to practice patience and kindness. Practice vulnerability.

JASMINE: I just didn't want to join a Dharma community until I found one that reflected my identity, and not because I simply needed to see reflections of myself everywhere all the time, even though more often than not that would be nice. I think that for those of us who are absconding—from the church and elsewhere, there has been a kind of compartmentalization of spirituality and sexuality. When I found a *sangha* that was full of women of color, mostly queer, it was suddenly OK to integrate the two in ways I had never experienced before. It was very healing. The idea that shame isn't a productive feeling in the work of liberation has been healing. The practice of lovingkindness, for example, asked me to look at the ways I was harboring an intense amount of anger, shame, and frustration for myself just because of who I wanted to be with or found myself attracted to. Of course that gets reinforced with personal reactions with people who are struggling with it themselves. At least having an intentional space to fully integrate all of who I was in a community of people, who are also doing that same work and are trying to heal together—I think that is absolutely transformative. I had a very unique experience for sure.

REV. ANGEL: Relationships to emotions are manipulated often in dharma communities by, in particular, not allowing, or squelching, anger as an expression.

LAMA ROD: Well, because it's ultimately uncomfortable, and in certain communities there's not a lot of inclusion. You have people of certain differences coming into the space, and they're angry, and all of a sudden I think a lot of white practitioners take responsibility for that and say, "I must be the cause of this. I don't want to deal with this." I think it triggers guilt in people.

And ultimately, we don't have strategies to work with our anger. Within radical activist communities, which I'm a member of, there's a worship of anger as being vital for community change. Now, I always have to go up against them and push back on that because I see people destroyed in anger and in rage. I have to go into the communities and say, "I think we have to acknowledge anger. We have to honor our anger, but we don't have to ground ourselves in anger as a momentum to create change."

I experience a lot of anger, but I'm not involved in activism because I'm pissed off. I'm involved because I want people to be happy. At the same time I admit that I experience anger all the time. And yet, I'm also motivated by trying to love in a way that's authentic and open. I'm struggling to see the nature of anger and to transform that anger into something that's about creating, not destroying.

REV. ANGEL: What would you say to practitioners who are entering into spaces that are predominantly white, and they're expressing their anger? Not necessarily rooting in it, but expressing their anger as part of conveying their experience?

LAMA ROD: There has to be the space for that. That's part of our experience. It's not that you're reacting to the anger, it's that you're connecting to it, which is very different than acting out of it for me. I look at anger, and I think: Anger was the first material I had to work with. Anger was so integrated into so many parts of my life that it took a lot of practice to uproot it. Under that anger was a lot of despair. I wasn't just pissed off just to be pissed off, I was pissed off because I was in so much despair and so much hopelessness.

I think for many communities of color, you get rooted in that hopelessness. There are no possibilities. There's no potential because we've been put in a certain place, and no one excels beyond that. We don't know how to contact that despair, until *sangha*, until people came to me and said, "Rod, I think you're pissed off." Then I would be like, "What in the hell do you know?" There was a lot of denial. That's how unintegrated rage was for me. It was under the radar. I was like, "I'm not angry. I'm not pissed off. I don't know what people are talking about!"

Then you're forced to look at it more and more. I began to see it. Over time, I began to own it as part of my experience.

It wasn't this extraordinary thing that only I was experiencing. Everyone was going through anger and despair and everything else. I wasn't so special.

I think what has helped me so much in my Dharma practice over these years is understanding that everyone is going through this. They may not be talking about it, but everyone's having similar experiences, because we all have mind, and mind has these experiences that we don't really know how to work with. If we did, the world would be a lot better place right now.

REV. ANGEL: The cultural value in this society has been if you don't know how to work with something, suppress it. Not only suppress it in yourself, suppress it in others, because if you don't suppress it in others, then it reminds you that you're suppressing it in yourself. That's part of what we're experiencing in the dharma communities—the suppression of emotion. Suppression of anger, in particular, is a way in which folks are not actually being controlled in terms of expressing their anger because they want to control you; it's that they want to control themselves.

One of the extraordinary things about liberation is that you do not feel the need to control things when you're free. And the freer you get, the less you feel the need to control. Because the illusory nature of control becomes clear to you. It's like, "I'm just making this up! I'm not actually controlling anything."

It's like your closet. It's not really clean in here; I just stuffed all the things in the closet, but now I'm anxious because the closet might burst open. I feel aware of the fact that there are things that are rotting in the closet, and they're causing a stench, and that stench is coming out. You may not even notice the smell, but I'm anxious, and I'm carrying and living under the burden of the anxiety of you becoming aware of the way in which I have put all of this stuff away. You know, when you're really hoarding, it's not just your furniture, your papers. Your shit is in there. So your shit is making a stink and you're anxious and you can't relax in your own skin. You feel triggered by someone else's presence. Not because they're doing something. It's because you have so much shit in your closet that you're holding back.

Having these conversations is liberating for us all. It's just opening the closet and saying, "OK, you know what is there. At least I can relax because now we know it's there and I don't have to be so on guard and fearful."

We're not talking enough about the fear that white folks hold as a result of race. I'm not talking about fear of colored people or fear of Black people. I'm talking about fear of one's own self, because you don't know how to have the conversation, because you feel shame about where you're located in that conversation, about how to locate yourself. We all feel shame when we're sitting on the cushion and stuff pops up in our head. We come to realize everything we think when no one is looking. What's liberating is once we are like, "This is what's going on. Now I understand my behavior, which seemed inexplicable at the time."

That's what happens; we get trapped. We behave in some way that's unconscious—unskillful behavior. Then we have to make meaning of it. If we don't make meaning of it, we'll be crazy, right? And we don't want to just think we're crazy, so we put words to it: I did that because you deserved it, because you showed up in a certain way, because you said something, you did something. You didn't behave the right way, and that's why I acted out.

What we're really saying is, "I don't know how to make sense of that behavior at all. That's frightening because it exposes the degree to which I'm out of control of myself. And that's way too scary to get involved with. So I'm just going to shut you down to shut it down, and then it's all shut down." There's no liberation there.

LAMA ROD: Many of us are really unstudied, unexamined, unquestioned. We're kind of operating on the sense of what we think we're talking about. We're not located within our experiences; we're not embodied. Because that really takes opening the closet and owning what's in there and being vulnerable around that.

I see that as work that everyone has to do, not just white folks. As a person that embodies a certain difference, for me there's been a practice of actually examining the parts of who and what I was that I habitually repressed. And I've had to connect to the sense of never feeling good enough. I've had to learn to create a language around that and to be vulnerable around that, because, at the end of the day—let's just say white supremacy is completely eradicated—that's great, but I'm still going to experience this sense of inferiority and this woundedness. I think we get distracted with trying to end white supremacy and oppression and racism, but there's still this work of healing that needs to be done for everyone, and we need to bring more attention to that piece.

Healing can be started now. I get pushback from people who say, "No! We need to end oppression. Or we need to end all these systems." I think that's how we get lost and distracted from the work of healing. I'm working to end racism and oppression, but at the same time I want to be liberated. I want to thrive. I want to be happy. How can we bring that ethic of healing back into our communities, into our *sanghas*, into our households, into our relationships, into our organizations?

REV. ANGEL: This is something that is challenging for people to understand—the notion of transforming society from the inside out. We're so in a framework of dichotomies that many people are like, "We have to do it outside first."

Understanding that part of our capacity to make change outside in a way that's actually generative comes from having done work inside so we can actually have empowerment that doesn't have to do with external conditions. We actually have models for it on the grand scale. All people admire Nelson Mandela for his refusal to be imprisoned in his own being, which enabled him to come out of prison after twenty-eight years, which then gave room for a level of change to happen on a social level.

So I'm not saying that we should only just work on ourselves and not do any work outside. But I think it's an immature view that believes "I have to do all of the external conditions and have them all change before I can be happy." I'm not willing to have my happiness wait for what might h appen out there.

We have to commit to our own liberation regardless of what happens outside. And paradoxically, that gives way to change happening outside. If I were having this conversation about anger and fire and brimstone and kill the whiteys, then I wouldn't be here, frankly. This is not what people would be invested in as a conversation. Certainly none of the white-run organizations would be. It's already a stretch that they're inviting us at all. [Laughter]

Lama Rod: I was just thinking about my own experience. But I better be careful. There are things I can't say if I want to get invited back. That's going to be the follow-up book to this project. [Laughter]

I'm thinking about my own liberation. I mean, I'm not liberated. Liberation is a process, and I think one of the first important things I had to do is stop believing in my inferiority. I had to actually stop believing what the world was trying to tell me I was. And I had to develop an experience of who I was on a very fundamental level through meditation practice. That's how I rebooted who and what I was, and so I have people in here from all parts of my life: childhood friends, high school friends, college friends, new friends. [Laughter]

There was a period where I just kind of crashed. And I made a choice: Do I restart with all the same old stuff, or do I restart and let go of what I don't need? Can I wipe the slate clean and then trust—and we find the same language in Christianity too—my life to a higher power? And that higher power for me was dharma.

I didn't have to wait for oppressive systems to be eradicated or overthrown. I made a choice, because I hit rock bottom. That I'm radical and anarchist follows many of those ideals and philosophies. That thing gets me as excited as listening to old speeches from Malcolm X and James Baldwin. James Baldwin was always advocating love and transformation. Those voices have somehow been lost.

So we have to start taking those teachings and writings seriously, because there's truth in that for us. We can have this rhetoric of overthrowing oppressive systems, but we have to balance that with the work of overthrowing the oppressive system operating internally that actually keeps us enslaved.

My principal teacher is Norlha Rinpoche, who is in his late seventies. He's a Tibetan from the generation of the Dalai

Lama, that same generation that either escaped Tibet when the Communists invaded in 1959 or who was interned in concentration camps. My teacher was, in fact, captured and interned in a concentration camp and escaped. So my teacher has an understanding of what it is to be oppressed, to escape genocide.

Being that I was one of his first Black senior students, he was always a step ahead of me. Meaning that, he's always been like, "You have an obligation to work with people who are like you. Because if you don't, you're wasting this opportunity to help people."

I'm so fortunate and privileged to have a teacher who's able to push me in that direction. Instead of saying, "You don't need to do that. You don't need to talk about race and sex." I go back and I say, "Rinpoche, you realize what I'm doing? I'm talking about all these things!" He was like, "Sure. Whatever."

REV. ANGEL: My experience of my teacher is very different than yours. I think that that's true for many people. Your teacher's Tibetan, and his relationship to racial constructs is entirely different, I'm imagining, than my teacher, a white lesbian in New York City.

And I was not having the "let me trust my teacher to point out what I need to know in order to fully experience myself." [I had] the opposite experience of feeling that my teacher was out of the place. And, given the immersive nature of racist constructs in this country, we're pointing out the things that she needed to point out in order to maintain her safety and her not working with what was there in the room. So I wanted to make sure that that's also clear. That it's ideal that we have teachers like yours, and if we don't, that we still are responsible for ourselves.

I had to make a choice to get my pointing-out instruction someplace else, to actually recognize I'm not getting pointed out to me what I need for my liberation, for my happiness—to actually unhook enough from my attachment to "this is my teacher and this is how it should be," to get what I needed.

Even though I had a lesbian teacher, I was still getting a white heteronormative frame of the Dharma. It didn't allow for a radical Dharma, and it let me, compelled me, or positioned me, I would say, inside a certain kind of privilege. Inside of that privilege one cannot be radical. It is like inside that privilege, that is the basic question to me about radical Dharma, and the theory of radical Dharma is that you have to let go of your privileges and turn the lenses of Dharma on the full scope and expression of your life. Not just inside of what your particular privilege is, whether that is whiteness or straightness or if you are in a dominant queer culture, which is maybe a privilege too. All of those things, so that was a live question for me. In this moment in history, our attention is rightfully turned to the history and ongoing policing of particularly Black and brown bodies. It is expressing itself as the state policing of these bodies, but it begs the question of where does the policing come from. Police forces are acting out a specific mandate of a social construct that we live inside of. The question we need to ask is where does this policing, whether it is policing queerness or Blackness, where does it come from and how does Dharma allow us to let go of an orientation that, because it is about acceptance, inherently undermines policing?

REMEMBERING LOVE: AN INFORMAL CONTEMPLATION ON HEALING

by Lama Rod Owens

You've got to learn to leave the table
When love's no longer being served.

—NINA SIMONE

Love takes off the masks that we fear we cannot live without
and know we cannot live within. I use the word "love" here
not merely in the personal sense but as a state of being, or a
state of grace—not in the infantile American sense of being
made happy but in the tough and universal sense of quest and
daring and growth.

—JAMES BALDWIN, *THE FIRE NEXT TIME*

Are you sure, sweetheart, that you want to be well? … Just
so's you're sure, sweetheart, and ready to be healed, cause
wholeness is no trifling matter. A lot of weight when you're
well.

—TONI CADE BAMBARA, *THE SALT EATERS*

REMEMBERING

When people ask me how I'm doing, I feel a little confused and pause for a moment. In my mind I want to talk about this deep sense of heaviness and despair that feels like mourning with and for the world. I want to say that a part of me doesn't feel good enough, that this was a feeling I was born into, trained in, and encouraged to accept—that I do not remember an experience before this.

Growing up, no one had ever talked about sexuality or sexual orientation. The boy knew he was gay by his mid-teens but did not have a language to express it. Even if he did, there was danger in saying the words.

After fifth grade, the boy had transferred to a mostly white school. He made white friends for the first time and began to notice that the white kids dressed better, always had money, had two parents at home and drove nice cars, took vacations, went to summer camps, could afford special study programs and tutors, were not in the free and reduced-price lunch program, and lived in multistory homes and nice neighborhoods. At that time, he lived in the projects with his mom, did not wear all name brand clothes, had gapped teeth; for the first time, he felt both poor and Black.

The boy hated riding the school bus home. Often he had to stand in the aisle, as the bus was always too crowded. As one of the younger students on the bus, he was bullied and harassed by older kids. Once someone jammed a pencil between his buttocks as if trying to penetrate him anally. Once, after an older student tripped passing him in the aisle, the student rammed his elbow across the boy's lower jaw. Though not in much pain, the boy wanted to cry. The only physical violence he had ever known was from other Black boys. He did not understand how anyone could feel safe around them.

One other afternoon the teen stopped at a convenience store to buy a snack. By the time he was walking out, the cops were waiting on him. The cashier had reported him as matching the description of someone who had been shoplifting there. The cops asked for ID and were respectful. The young man kept thinking how he didn't do anything to deserve this. Afterward the boy raced home, paranoid, and locked himself in his room. He had no idea what was wrong with him. He was sobbing, terrified, and ashamed for being both.

The young man had been larger bodied most of his life. He was labeled "fat" in the gay male community. Because of this, he felt judged, marginalized, and devalued. He felt unattractive and undesirable. He felt that he was not thin or handsome enough to be loved. Those he was attracted to were not attracted to him. Once, after chatting with another man online using a profile picture portraying him as thinner than he was, he met him in person. The man took one look at him and explained bluntly to the young man, "You need to be honest with yourself," and walked away. It took the young man years to love and trust his body after that.

He was new to Buddhism and was sitting his first ten-day intensive retreat. During the question-and-answer period after a dharma talk, he explained to the white male teacher that he felt lonely and marginalized in the *sangha* as the only person of color. The teacher suggested that this was something the young man struggled with outside of the *sangha*. The young man agreed. The teacher advised him to just sit with what he was feeling. The young man wanted more and did sit with the feelings and knew that the *sangha* and that teacher were not safe for him.

I want to say how much I am feeling my personal trauma compounded from lifetimes of psychological and emotional violence endured and held not only by myself, but by many generations before me and passed on to me without my consent. I want to say that it breaks my heart that we have to tell little Black boys they will have to survive being Black and male in a time and place that chooses not to hold them warmly or kindly.

And then there was that afternoon when Velma had done her best. As a brown-bodied woman engaged in the work of social change, she could not continue any longer. Activism, racism, misogyny, marriage, and work had taken its toll. The struggle for mental, physical, and spiritual liberation had left her body worn, spirit weak, and her mind sick and trembling. As a reward for her efforts to take her own life, she found herself barely wrapped in a hospital gown, waiting for hands to be laid on her.

Minnie came as healer. Velma resisted. She couldn't decide if she was ready to be healed. Finally, Minnie checked in: "Are you sure, sweetheart, that you want to be well? … Just so's you're sure, sweetheart, and ready to be healed, cause wholeness is no trifling matter. A lot of weight when you're well."²

On Thursday, June 18, 2015, I woke to the mourning of nine slaughtered Black bodies in Charleston, South Carolina. The brutality of the massacre was an act of terrorism in my own heart, breaking it into a million little pieces of aching. I felt that Toni Cade Bambara's classic novel, *The Salt Eaters*, was reading me. I was feeling a little like Velma in the novel, lost, frustrated, and resisting. Broken. I held onto Minnie's appeal to Velma

---

² Toni Cade Bambara, *The Salt Eaters, 1st Vintage Contemporaries ed.* (New York: Random House, 1992), 10.

as if she were speaking to me. I wanted and needed healing. I craved for Minnie's hands to be laid on me. I needed to be liberated. This morning I wanted to be whole. I wanted the privilege of the weight of what it meant to be well. I wanted to know what it meant to be healed.

When did I decide I wanted to carry this weight?

DESCRIBING TRAUMA

If I am to speak of healing, then I must first speak of trauma. When I speak of trauma, I speak of experiences that impact how we relate to ourselves and to others around us. These experiences, mostly related to our emotional capacities and also called woundedness, hurting, aching, or pain, refer to both the subtle and gross experiences that make it very difficult to feel confident, safe, or to experience happiness, well-being, and balance. In this understanding of trauma, trauma can be healed. Through the cultivation of awareness practice, we can learn to identify our traumas, accept them, investigate them, and learn to let them go in concert with sustaining heart practices such as lovingkindness (*metta*), taking and sending (*tonglen*), and compassion practices.

In my experience, trauma is the creation of a context that does not privilege my deepest desire to return home and inhabit my own agency and body, but instead triggers disembodiment and a loss of awareness of the body and its experiences. Thus, trauma becomes a cyclical experience of continuous unfolding, of continuous movement through places without consent as it perpetuates terror, despair, hopelessness, and disconnection. It is a voyage that never docks at any port, but is suspended, unexamined. When I am feeling my own trauma,

I find that I am also seeking some way to find ground, an anchor.

GIVING VOICE TO HEALING

Healing is difficult for me to talk about, to neatly conceptualize in a language that communicates my relationship to what I consider a process of slow but intentional liberation. I am nervous and anxious to speak of healing in spaces and places that are suspicious of what it means to heal. I know that sometimes we distrust healing because it means that we have to imagine a different way of being in the world beyond our anger, woundedness, or despair. Moreover, we believe that to move beyond these hurts means that we can no longer be attuned to the suffering of communities and people struggling for justice, equality, or basic visibility. Or maybe because we feel that healing means forgetting that we have been hurt, oppressed, and that there is an oppressor who should and must be held accountable for their violence.

Perhaps we think healing means weakness, that we are no longer strong when we are healed or that healing zaps our super-human ability of being pissed off and agitated, which we think keeps us conscious and present. We have learned that anger is a part of the work of social liberation, that being angry is what motivates and drives us. To a certain extent this is true. However, I believe that the true blessing of anger is how it can indicate an imbalance in our experience and in the world around us. But we have to be very clear: Anger is not about creating or building up. That is the work of loving.

Or maybe we believe that the right to healing is only for those who have been hurt and oppressed, and we are upset to consider that the one who hurts and oppresses is in just as much need of healing. It is hard for us to consider that if the oppressor is healed, then maybe he or she would not reproduce so much violence.

When I hear folks' distrust of healing, especially in marginalized and traumatized communities, I hear the subtle and nuanced workings of internalized oppression that distract us from imagining liberation that is not about struggling against systems and regimes but about transcending the trauma of struggling and residing in the nature of who we are as people who can be psychically free though physically bound. For when I define healing as freedom, I mean to interrogate how I am slave to my own self-depreciation fueled by internalized oppression.

I want to say that these days when I see dead Black men on TV, I see myself; watching bombs being dropped on communities of brown people anywhere feels like bombs falling on my head. I want to say that sometimes the experience of my skin color is one akin to a desperate need to rip off a burning outfit.

I speak about healing because I need you to know that if it were not for healing, I would not be alive. I would not have survived my own intersectionality in a time and place that struggle to hold difference warmly or kindly. Identity is wounding only because we survive in places where difference remains invisible instead of being seen and celebrated. Not only that, many of us do not know how to celebrate our difference because we have been taught to repress difference in an effort to gain social privileges or, to put it another way, access to the master's house. Because I survived my intersectionality, I am showing up a survivor of conditions that were not set by me but that I still must endure. Yet, for this to be understood, we must be shown what is required to make the possible possible.

WHAT IS LOVE?

Whatever we think love is, love often isn't. It took me years of practice to understand what love was. I had always heard about it and had often been told of its importance. I knew that I was still alive because of the love of my mother and others. But love was often something I associated with fear. Once, a friend confided that self-love was something their mother had taught them wasn't possible and that my friend should just learn to live with that truth. When I heard this, something inside of me rebelled and I felt sad. I felt upset hearing that my friend believed this from their mother. I felt upset as well because, though I believed in self-love, I knew that there was more self-hate than love for me at that time. In that moment, I vowed to learn to love myself through what seemed like thick folds of self-hate.

Love is the wish for myself and others to be happy. Love transcends our need to control the recipient of love. I love not because I need something in return. I love not because I want to be loved back, but because I see and understand love as being an expression of the spaciousness I experience when I am challenging my egoic fixation by thinking about the welfare of others. I go where I am loved. I go where I am allowed to express love. In loving, I have no expectations.

Healing is being situated in love. Healing is not just the courage to love, but to be loved. It is the courage to want to be happy not just for others, but for ourselves as well. It is interrogating our bodies as an artifact of accumulated traumas and doing the work of processing that trauma by developing the capacity to notice and be with our pain. If we are to heal, then we must allow our awareness to settle into and integrate with the pain and discomfort that has been habitually avoided. We cannot medicate the pain away. We embrace it, and in so doing establish a new relationship with the experience. We must see that there is something that must be befriended. This is the true nature of our experience, and in finally approaching this experience we contact basic sanity.

Too often love has meant violence in the form of our manipulation and control. Many of us have learned at an early age that we are only lovable if we meet certain conditions and expectations. The message from our environments has been something like, "You can only be loved if you do _____ or if you are _____."

Because love is conditional, we develop the art of performing in order to get the love that we need without understanding that we, by nature of having been born, have a natural right to love and receive love. We are controlled by others when we are dependent on their love and thus struggle to meet the demands that they place on us to receive that love.

When we attempt to love out of our woundedness, then our loving is only violence. Love needs spaciousness in our minds to manifest and endure. If there is no space, it is very difficult to experience a sense of confidence and trust in our own bodies and experience. When none of this is present, our movement and interactions in the world are limited and selfish. Our hurt is our deep identification with a self that can and is experiencing pain. When we are identifying like this, then our actions are more about protecting ourselves than generating authentic concern for others. We see the world around us as antagonistic. Everything becomes a threat. Because of this perceived threat, we often find ourselves in a heightened state of responsiveness, always reacting and attacking. In this way, we are protecting ourselves against others and further acting out of a frustration of never feeling comfortable. Our acting perpetuates suffering for others and thus violence is reproduced.

COMING OUT AND RISKING LOVE

Many of us have come out multiple times, in many ways. There are always risks with coming out. Often that risk is losing the love from others. When I think of coming out, I am always reminded of coming out as a gay person. When I came out to my mother, I was twenty-four. She was the first family member I came out to. I had been living in Boston, in therapy, and nowhere near being interested in practicing dharma. With my therapist, I had decided to formally start coming out to family. I had started coming out to friends at the end of high school and was completely out in college, but I had not made it a priority to officially come out to family. I figured if they found out, they found out. If not, oh well. In any case, I had decided with my therapist that I would tell my mom the truth during my visit home.

The time chose me strategically. We were on our way back from church one afternoon. We stopped at a red light and something said, "It's time." So, I stepped over the ledge and hoped the net would catch me. I told her that I wanted to tell her that I was gay because I wanted her to know. There was a pause and then a question from her as to how I knew. My response was about my natural attraction to and loving of other men. Upon arriving home, we observed the great Black folk tradition of sitting on the front porch as she simply said that nothing had changed between us and that she still loved me and that she just wanted me to be safe. I think the greatest fear we have coming out about anything is the possibility that we will not be loved by those we need love from. There would have been significant woundedness if my mother said that she could not accept me or love me because of my sexuality. I was very fortunate to receive love from a mother who, in that one instant, chose not to commit violence by restricting her love but chose to love more intensely, thereby becoming an agent of my further healing.

HEALING AND SHOWING UP

When I suffered severe depression, the easiest thing to do was hide it. You become quite skilled in distracting others from focusing on you and your suffering. This is possible because most people are not interested really in how others are suffering and certainly not interested in their own suffering. There's no judgement here. Suffering is difficult and tough.

It's complicated and very uncomfortable. Most of us master the game of distracting ourselves and avoiding vulnerability. I kept my disease to myself and found myself quietly slipping away, disappearing. Not many people noticed.

Healing is movement and work toward wholeness. Healing is never a definite location but something in process. It is the basic ordinary work of staying engaged with our own hurt and limitations. Healing does not mean forgiveness either, though it is a result of it. Healing is knowing our woundedness; it is developing an intimacy with the ways in which we suffer. Healing is learning to love the wound because love draws us into relationship with it instead of avoiding feeling the discomfort.

Healing means we are holding the space for our woundedness and allowing it to open our hearts to the reality that we are not the only people who are hurt, lonely, angry, or frustrated. We must also release the habitual aggression that characterizes our avoidance of trauma or any discomfort. My goal is to befriend my pain, to relate to it intimately as a means to end the suffering of desperately trying to avoid it. Opening our hearts to woundedness helps us to understand that everyone else around us carries around the same woundedness.

And while I continue to heal myself, I continue to hurt myself. Using racism as an example, though I struggle to use my practice to bring awareness of internalized oppression manifesting as racial trauma, I am also struggling to see how I am also an agent of white supremacy as I unconsciously value white bodies as aesthetically pleasing and cleaner, while simultaneously seeing my body and other brown and Black bodies as less attractive. How my internalizing of white supremacy urges me to be on guard when passing another Black male on the sidewalk, to be embarrassed when other Black or brown bodies are acting out in public spaces, or to hide my rage and despair in order to keep white people cozy.

In my healing I am also mourning. Sometimes I am in despair. Mourning and despair are very private matters. It is my acknowledgment that there is suffering. It is my honoring of my discomfort as well as the discomfort of everyone else in the world. One of the blessings of lovingkindness practice is that the heart remains raw, sensitive, and open to pain. As I am mourning, I am remembering my commitment engendered in my bodhisattva vow, not just to achieve enlightenment to free all beings, but to hold the space for the pain of beings in my practice as I hold my own. When we begin to confront our trauma, we give permission for others to do the same. This is the work of the contemporary bodhisattva. Ultimately, holding the space for the pain to be present in our experience and our capacity to do this eventually inform the effectiveness of our healing and will make us the healer.

HEALING AND LINEAGE

The most profound practice I have ever been taught by my teachers is simply letting my shit fall apart, developing the courage to sit with all of my rough edges, the ugliness, the destructive and suffocating story lines I have perpetuated about myself, and letting go of the same suffocating storylines others maintain about me. It is this practice that sometimes involves sitting in my room alone and letting the tears and pain have their way. But it is also the practice of learning to smile and lean into the hard stuff, allowing it to wake me up to make better decisions.

There is healing through lineage. Sometimes I cannot describe what I mean by lineage. Yet my experience of lineage is about being received and held within a field of continuous loving-warmth, kindness, and compassion. It is about the transhistorical gifting of unconditional acceptance. It is the inheritance of permission to transcend the silliness of living out of the confinement of the ego-bound self. It is the permission to sprout wings and take to the sky as others have before me. Their example becomes the heart of the legacy you will leave behind.

My lineage is also intersectionality. It is evoking and honoring all the little pieces of who I am, that which inform the way I show up. I summon my identities like I summon the ancestors and demand that they speak truth to me because if they do not, I am a living lie. To be a lie is to go against my purpose as a body who holds and shares dharma.

Before I give a dharma talk I am usually in silence for some period of time, feeling into the community, leaning into what those present are projecting, trying to hold the space for my fears and anxieties. It is a tender period for me. I need to know that I am being held by lineage. I need to know that before I open my mouth, I am speaking lineage. I take the time to call upon my dharma lineage, evoking the names of the great masters such as Tilopa, Naropa, Milarepa as well as the living-flesh teachers I am devoted to in this life.

I also evoke the blessing of Tara, the female Buddha of compassion, to support me as I lean into my own discomfort so that I can lean into the suffering I sense around me. Often I imagine the essence of my lineage in the form of Tara descending into me like I am possessed.

I *am* possessed by Tara. It is moving and poignant. Through the blessing of Tara and my lineage, I am there, with people, in my body, being with and loving all the parts of my identity because these parts have taught me how to be kind, passionate, fierce, and tender at the same time. Tara holds this Black queer body in such compassion that I do not feel the need to apologize for anything. She is the woman holding my hand so that I may hold the hand of those who have come to me to be held. At some point I become the woman, the mother. This is when lineage is moving in me.

TAKING, SENDING, AND RECEIVING AS HEALING

Tonglen means taking and sending, or can be described as replacing our selves for others. It is a transformative practice. We could say that this practice is one of radical expansion in which we are challenging the boundaries we erect and giving permission for these boundaries to be dissolved in our increasing care and concern for others around us. This care and concern is the deepening of our own inherent compassion, which is both the recognition of suffering in ourselves and others and the aspiration to alleviate this suffering. *Tonglen* allows me to enter into a kind of intimacy with my own woundedness and offers me a way to stay connected to my experience. When I am in tune to my discomfort, I am less likely to avoid your discomfort. Or to put it another way: when I am able to show up to my suffering, I can also show up to yours.

When I practice lovingkindness, I need to remember that I am cared for. I need to remember that my feelings of being lonely, isolated, and unlovable are essentially the illusions perpetuated by my ego fixation. When I am practicing, I wish to experience the deepest well-being and happiness, and gradually I begin wishing that others experience the same thing. In this way I begin the courageous and great work of loving myself and extending that same love to as many people as I can.

EPILOGUE

But I was very lucky because as I slipped away I began waking up more to what was happening and refused to disappear. My journey led me into meditation, Buddhism, nutrition, physical fitness, and the world of alternative healing. I'm lucky to have cured myself with the help of healers and my teachers, and I'm lucky to be alive. I only write this because many of you are suffering and feel helpless and stigmatized. Many of you will not articulate your suffering and will not seek help. I especially write to Black folks who historically suffer from many forms of mental illness that remain undiagnosed. We have to start talking about our struggle, especially in light of managing and/or transcending this suffering. I also write to remember everyone who didn't make it and are not making it. But yes, I have survived depression. I'm not ashamed to say that. If you need help, I'm here.

In the end, what I have survived is not myself but people, systems, and institutions that have used physical, emotional, spiritual, and other forms of psychic violence to insist that I should be something other than myself. It is not my particular intersectionality that has been my suffering, but rather the suffering that comes from my intersectionality not being honored, accepted, or even celebrated. I am a survivor of perpetual invisibility, which has often resulted in me doubting my self-worth, integrity, and general health. Thus, part of my trauma has been believing that I do not matter and that the world doesn't care. In my experience, invisibility becomes a kind of murder. For communities I identify with that are struggling to be seen, it is genocide.

I want to say that I will continue smiling at police folks. And understand that when you blame me for your unexamined issues, I will still want you to be happy. When you call me a name meant to hurt me, I will try not to take it personally as you are also trying to express your own despair. I want to say that I am tired of struggling and am practicing being where I want to be. In my mind, I am saying all this, but I haven't figured out how to get this across. I apologize for my confusion.

In the end, my healing has been learning to see myself and to celebrate myself. It is interrogating the stories about how I do not matter and choosing to let go of those narratives and engage in the necessary and revolutionary work, self-love, and liberation. Through self-loving, I can know my aching and choose not to show up in reaction to the aching, but to show up being informed by my aching in a way that wakes me up to the reality that everyone else around me is aching as well. I am not alone in needing to be seen.

But I also want to say that despite my uneasiness in the world, I'm OK and that I'm fine with feeling angry and sad because that's a part of my humanity and I am learning to have more space to be human. I want to say that I try not to blame others so much and that I am trying to lean into the heaviness and despair, that I'm trying to stay open and not shut down. I want to say that my speechlessness in reaction to the ugliness around me is slowly giving way to a choice to honor life with silent contemplation.

In the end, I am no longer the little boy having to hold the potential violence of those in stress around him, or the little boy who is afraid to claim his love for other men, or the pre-teen who is challenged to make meaning out of race and class, or the young teen terrified of riding the bus, or the young man othered because of his body type, or the man who is told that his feelings of marginalization are his issue not the issue of a *sangha* steeped in white-supremacist cultural norms. I am no longer these people, but I remember their stories. They made me who I am. Because of them, I have earned my dharma. I have been blessed with a testimony.

Again, I remember Velma. I used to be Velma. Minnie came to me not once, but many times over. Her words were always the same: "Are you sure, sweetheart, that you want to be well? … Just so's you're sure, sweetheart, and ready to be healed, cause wholeness is no trifling matter. A lot of weight when you're well."

Perhaps what I have come to understand, finally, is that somehow I have become the one I have always wanted. This is why I do the things that I do. There is a fierce love that wakes me up every morning, that makes me tell my stories, refuses to let me apologize for my being here, blesses me with the capacity to be silent, alone, and grieving when I most need to be. You have to understand that this is what I mean when I say healing.

May all beings be seen, held kindly, and loved. May we all one day surrender to the weight of being healed.

RADICALIZING DHARMA DREAMS

by Jasmine Syedullah, PhD

On truth's path, wise is mad, insane is wise. In love's way, self and other are the same. Having drunk the wine, my love, of being one with you, I find the way to Mecca and Bodhgaya are the same.

—#302, FROM RUMI'S *KOLLIYAAT-E SHAMS-E TABRIZI*, EDITED BY BADIOZZAMAN FOROUZANFAR (TEHRAN, AMIR KABIR, 1988)

All that is deeply true is a paradox.

—REV. ANGEL KYODO WILLIAMS, SENSEI

Why not sit? Why not stop the Ferris wheel only to sit on a rainbow-colored steel horse for a while? Neither people-watching nor waiting, but just sitting? To find peace? To escape the hustle and bustle of this life? Its rushed hours and heartbreaks? Its delusions and disappointments? Perhaps because in the act of sitting there is nothing to be attained?

STRANGERS AT THE GATES

There came a time in my own practice when the lofty dreams and abstract ideals that originally compelled me toward a cushion, a mat, a *sangha*, or tradition of wisdom teachings, began to dissolve. I didn't find nirvana on my cushion. I did, however, find something, in the depths of the night, surrounded by police, sitting on a cushion while holding vigil with thousands before the gates of a federal prison. It was the evening of December 12th. The year was 2005. I had traveled with my *sangha* from Oakland to the foothills of Marin to participate in a talk led by Rev. angel and Jack Kornfield at Spirit Rock. At that point it was the most racially mixed, densely populated Buddhist gathering I'd ever seen. After the talk several of us bundled up with blankets, hats, scarves, and warm jackets with our meditation cushions in tow and headed to San Quentin in protest of the state-sanctioned execution of a man named Stanley Tookie Williams. Williams had been arrested, convicted, and sentenced to death in the early '80s. He had spent more than twenty years on death row. He had entered prison the co-founding leader of one of the most notorious gangs in America, the Crips. By the time of his execution he had become a Nobel Peace Prize nominee five times over for his violence-prevention efforts with urban youth. He was globally celebrated by noteworthy public figures and respected by national progressive organizations. That night he was to suffer death by lethal injection.

We heard the chants before we saw their faces. Hundreds packed the vacant streets that led to the prison gates. The shouts cut through the cool nighttime air, calling us all to come together. We rolled in chanting. Bathed in the intermittent light of hard flashes from the big local news cameras and the flickering glow of white-stemmed candles that cast an eerie light across a sea of unfamiliar faces, we, the urban *sangha*, joined a motley crew of anarchists, preachers, politicians, white liberals, Black Muslims, communists, hip-hop moguls, and blue-clad Crips. We were flanked by quiet rows of surprisingly passive police. We were flowing together like a river toward the gates of the prison. *We are,* I thought silently, *the strange bedfellows of the next social revolution.*

Our walking meditation winded along a seemingly endless pathway until we arrived at a clearing, lines of protestors spilling out of formation and pooling in dense crowds before the police-lined and barricaded West Gate of California's oldest institution of incarceration, San Quentin State Prison, home to the state's only gas chamber and death row.

We were there for Williams. Not because, like Troy Davis, we believed he was innocent. Though many believed he was not guilty of the crimes for which he had been sentenced, and, though I had no doubt he had contributed violent acts, I was also certain those actions should not cost him his life. The propensity for violence for which the law held him accountable was not his alone to own. The historical conditions of its formation rose alongside the globalization of the U.S. empire that sowed the seeds of 9/11—arming Afghan mercenaries with military weapons and training them to fight Soviet soldiers in a war without end. Williams was no saint, but like many of us he was invested in healing himself and the community he had helped to harm. For the last several years of his incarceration he spent his time writing children's books, giving public talks, and creating online educational resources designed to prevent young men like him from following the path he himself had chosen. Tookie's was the hard-won kind of auto-correct that reflected our own need for another chance, for forgiveness, for something with longer-term visions of justice than retributive violence can afford, for something beyond the cycle of punishment, exile, and annihilation we erect around those whose presence poses a clear and present danger to our sense of safety.

The evening felt surreal, like midnight might strike and some old tension might break, give way to the improbable. Maybe a miracle. Posters bearing his words and his face filled the air. The voices of the few capital-punishment supporters were consumed by a sea of Williams's advocates, drowned out by our fiery calls for his immediate release from death row. We placed meditation cushions in a circle on the concrete pavement and sat in the midst of the crowd. Bringing stillness into the roar of five thousand from the coolness of the ground.

In the silence I could feel it all. The grief. The rage. Injustice has a flavor, a smell. It chokes the breath and burns the gut. It rises through the body like poison, like fire. I sat until I couldn't sit any more. My wavering voice joined the others. At the eleventh hour, phone in hand, I scrolled the news updates in search of the latest, a sign that the fate of the condemned may still be stayed. "Without an apology and atonement for these senseless and brutal killings, there can be no redemption," a quote from then Governor Schwarzenegger read. I braced myself. Tookie was being punished for dedicating his children's book about the danger of gangs to political prisoner George Jackson and Black Panther Party leader Huey P. Newton. He was being killed as much for his affiliation with enemies of the state, as he was for choosing self-defense over violating the trust of those who put their trust in him. Rather than informing on the internal affairs of gang life, he was choosing to align himself with the nameless—those with no selves to defend from the threat of death row. I clasped hands with strangers. We wrapped each other's rage up with our voices. We stood as one terrific body of dissent against the cold and death, armed with nothing but the fullness of our attention, our witness, our whole selves.

In the earliest hour of morning, more than half an hour past midnight, it was announced. Stanley Tookie Williams had become the twelfth person to be legally executed by the State of California since the reinstatement of that brutal and dehumanizing practice in 1978. Though his personal transformation was not enough to convince Governor Schwarzenegger that his life was worth saving, it was not an event that passed unnoticed.

Self-defense, in this context, is, like violence, never an individual act. Self-defense becomes possible through the cooperation of many forces, people, ideas, movements, and wars. Instead of the image of self-defense we are used to, something like a high-noon standoff at the O.K. Corral, it might be more like a scene from a horror movie, something like a zombie feeding frenzy. An early scene. A mob attack in a populated area. The frantic funneling of senseless force against an immediately imposing and clearly eminent threat. Are they mad or just hungry? Everyone fears the zombies. No one suspects the humans are zombicidal.

INTRODUCTION TO MEDITATION

So why sit? It couldn't save Stanley. It didn't start a revolution. At the beginning I picked up sitting as a means to an end. Another way to achieve. The best way to arrest what Augusto Boal calls the cops in your head. I was using meditation to police the police so to speak, adopting their instruments of surveillance, punishment, exile, and control in service to my own liberation. It was not working. It gave me a reason, a purpose, a way out of my head but not a way out of my habits of self-isolation, the deepest lie of this heteronormative hero-obsessed culture, believing that the only one I could rely on to save me was myself. What was first a refuge became its own prison. After sitting with those who stood for Tookie, my deep and abiding suspicion that prisons cannot keep us safe and that criminalization was not in the common interest of justice became more than a cause. It became a calling. Being fully in the stillness was not about self-isolation or self-help but about standing in radical relationship with all that stillness holds, with all the grief, all the loss, all the loneliness, and for a moment no matter what, standing *with* it rather than rushing to reason it away, arrest it, lock it in a box, and throw away the key. Nothing can be truly destroyed this way. Not even the dead stay buried.

When I first came to Rev. angel's *sangha* and the fearless-warrior practice she was developing, it made me so uncomfortable that she had to teach it to me about ten times. The instruction to keep our eyes slightly open rather than completely closed was not just difficult to remember; it was irritating. I preferred instead to seal myself off from the world, content that the dharma dreams that danced behind blissfully pulled-lid screens were what was working for me. It took months to unlearn the habits of sitting in isolation I had picked up from the academy. Even after much instruction, I was struggling to notice what I was doing, stop, and start again. In order to embody the practice of sitting in meditation as if I were on the edge of a battlefield awaiting my cue to combat rather than atop a mountain in the clouds, I had to come to see what all I feared to face in my practice, in myself.

The older practices were not wrong; they were, however, alibis in my own desire to appear unflappable, while actually managing to be still hiding from myself. The meditative stance of the fearless warrior was not that of the Christian monk, nor the Eastern ascetic. She was fearless warrior living in a city, not a monastic alone on a mountain. Her senses were poised for action, fully present, alive, relaxed, embodied, alert. Thus, her eyes remain slightly open and cast down at a forty-five-degree angle with the ground, gazing gently ahead in order to maintain detached connection with the world and an attitude of readiness to rejoin it whenever the need arose. In the practice we move in response to bells rather than bullets. In the service we learn to invite the sound of the bell as an extension of the practice, not as an anxious exit strategy. We lead the chant because a strong, steady pace must be set and a container for others must be held, not because we excel in mastering protocol and serving up convincing performances of leadership.

There can be an implicit shadiness in the retreat to monastic life within the cosmopolitan exigencies of urban existence. A kind of entitled solipsism and air of self-righteousness that can accompany the dharma talk that romanticizes the merits of meditation as a priority and thus as justification for withdrawing from direct forms of engagement with things as they are—with injustice, inequity, pain, injury, disease, violence, apathy, ignorance, neglect. When we move as one in the practice hall, we are peaceful. This is not necessarily so when we leave it behind for the hard ground of public protest. The fear of mob mentality in our modern, civilized culture is a curious one. We can trace it back to Cold War anxieties or fear of slave uprisings. At the end of the day, the assumption that crowds acting in concert need to be controlled taints our everyday connections to feeling each other—to feeling interconnected. It makes us fear those we learn to call strangers. It makes us strange in the presence of the unknown.

A sitting practice is about more than seeking peace. It is self-defense, more than a dream state of good intentions that are "useful" for becoming less wound up in the spin cycle of day-to-day life. It is also the most powerful weapon in the face of insurmountable horror, a way to stop even the cops, in the midst of everything and stand at the gates of the prison as the many made one to confront the coming threat head on. We might not save anyone. We might have to bear witness to an execution. But we were there. We were taking note, paying attention, and, because we were there, it was not a moment that went unnoticed.

"Do you want to be asleep or awake?" the teacher asked, and the student allowed her eyes to open slightly. She drew them down. Gently casting a forty-five-degree angle with the ground, already more steady, more present to herself, ready to meet whatever might arise. In following the instruction, I dared my dharma practice to wake up, come out of isolation and become animated, to come out of a space of suspended good faith, to become a practice that lived both on and off the cushion, bringing me more present to myself and closer into the world. The fearless warrior practice trained me to sit with all my internal cops and unconscious prisoners, the guilty, the innocent, the ghosts, the saints, and the monsters. It gave me a chance to see all their strange and idiosyncratic machinations and take note of their marionette-like possession of my sense of self, my disgust, my shame, my self-preservation.

I began to study the waxing and waning of my own prison-house of selves like a beloved guardian until my own attachments to their coming and going became increasingly more familiar and less startling to me. The steady routine of my own punitive reactions to my missteps became more readily recognizable over time as a discrete series of feelings and activities I rely on and engage for real reasons instead of a set of crimes to be controlled and corrected. The tendency to police becomes less compulsive, more conscious with practice. Abandoned pieces, places and people cut off become inhabitable, hospitable, less hostile. What if we went there? Away from reliance on police, cuffs, kill shots, and cages? What if we flocked? What if we crowded conventions of justice with conduct becoming a more collective vision of freedom. Do we police because we fear we can be savages? Do our barricades from each other belie the blinds that keep us strangers to ourselves?

ANY GIVEN SOMEDAY

It is not enough to know we want freedom. We have to practice it. We have to be able to live it out together. Remind each other how messy practice can be but rally each other to keep going for it. It might not make sense. It might not appear reasonable. Knowing we want freedom is a practice in presence not fortune-telling, not story-telling. There are no guarantees. No gold stars for having arrived on the other side perfectly unscathed. No chance of anyone nailing a perfect landing anyhow.

The skillfulness required to still all forms of policing, punishment, and separation we typically bring to our practices of liberation is not a matter of mastery. Our individual attempts to brace ourselves from the presence of each other are messy, angry, and hurtful. We throw up borders of separation to keep ourselves safe and somehow manage to find ourselves more miserable.

So often the ways I hear folk talk about practice and represent its value are wrapped up in the idea that freedom is a means to an end, especially within the U.S. context, given our particular historical relationship to freedom being legally and morally bound up in discourses of property, entitlement, mastery, exchange, dispossession, and exclusion. What if freedom is not a means to an end full of more comforts than this moment, right now? We may yet be further inconvenienced along the way.

In January 2015 I sat in a *zendo* at Brooklyn Zen Center. It was nearly MLK Day. We chanted the words of his speech, *A Time to Break Silence*, in unison. Calling out in one voice his words, "True compassion is more than flinging a coin to a beggar; it is not haphazard and superficial. It comes to see that an edifice which produces beggars needs restructuring. A true revolution of values will soon look uneasily on the glaring contrast of poverty and wealth ... and say, 'This is not just.' ... The Western arrogance of feeling that it has everything to teach others and nothing to learn from them is not just. A true revolution of values will lay hands on the world order and say of war, 'This way of settling differences is not just.'"[3]

Singing together "We Shall Overcome" gave me great hope, because it was clear that here in this space we were claiming the dream of liberation as something other than a good intention or a romantic destination. The navel-gazing attention on the self I had come to expect to be fractured was being very explicitly redirected to a call for wholeness and an end to injustice. In Rev. angel's talk that day she reminded us all of the importance of not getting caught up in the hand-wringing that comes with worrying over what we ought to do with the obstacles to our liberation. That we stop checking out, check in and work together to try to do things in ways we might

---

[3] Martin Luther King Jr. and Lewis V. Baldwin, *"In a Single Garment of Destiny": A Global Vision of Justice* (Boston: Beacon Press, 2012).

not yet know how to is more important than knowing the right thing to do. Bodies are dropping while we're debating. She said the incessant preoccupation with trying to name the first thing to do can be itself a hindrance. Radicalizing dharma dreams of liberation into political practice is no guarantee that we'll be free from spaces of confusion, pain, separation, and suffering. We must begin to practice sitting together to stand together.

The teacher also talked about remembering to make room at the table of our suffering and sadness for joy. Deep in my heart. Someday. I believe. Singing the song of uncertainty in this instance was anything but reason for misery or resignation. It was a triumphant testament to the glory of love, a way of making room for that which we can't yet know and can't wait for any longer. Love is liberation, and liberation is love. Especially when you are pretty sure you cannot win. We can still wrap each other up in our chanting voices, add our radical love to the feelings of despair. Keeping our eyes open, senses alert. You never really know what might happen. This is how I want to learn to want to be free. Not in search for a perfect monastic mountaintop far away from the problems of the world, but on the ready, among the many, singing each other's radical wisdom, waking up to ourselves, our dead, to their hearts and hunger, to their dreams of someday, I believe.

As an activist academic I often cringe at such touchy-feely sentiment. There is no time for feelings. The endless crunch of priorities punishes me for stopping long enough to notice my rage wreaking havoc on my body. It is not an accident. In the rush of the endless ways we find ourselves lost, late, behind, functioning beneath our best intentions and expectations; "I didn't sit today" does not generally rise to the top ten list of reasons we find ourselves lying awake in the middle of the night. So, why sit?

A friend wrote me the other day, telling me of her upsetting encounter with egoism in the academy, and she said, "I don't know if I can last long in this world." I responded not with blind optimism, but with the improvisational spirit of one for whom liberation from suffering is not an entitlement but a practice. "What if the thing that has to go, because something's got to give, is anxiety itself?" I said. What if managing the fear of falling off this Ferris wheel—or anticipating its flying off its supports—is just too exhausting? Instead of propping one's self up on lofty expectations or dropping the ball on our responsibility to ourselves, to our work, to being present, to caring for each other, what would it look like to cut off our attachment, that hardwired sense of obligation to staying stressed? The Ferris wheel can't stop, won't stop, but we can. We can just sit on a rainbow-colored steel horse for a while and just watch the wildings of fear wreak havoc on our sense of safety. Ride and watch. Witness and wilding.

"We are experimenting with new strategies for survival," I told my friend. "Their efficacy is necessarily not reflected in dominant culture, and yet throughout history we hear stories of folks refusing competition in precisely this way and daring to walk together to another rhythm. The fact that this bluesy fugitive rhythm does not 'work' in this world is proof of its success. We just have to remember we are not alone in this journey. We sit to practice being with ourselves so we can better sit, love, and live with those who will show up and help us along the way."

We are not yet drones. We can still clear some cobwebs, tend to some wounds, and invite our bodies into practices of looking.

We can cut through all that separates us from ourselves and ourselves from each other with a breath, maybe two. We can believe, broaden ground, offer new direction. Even under slavery I am told the people could fly. As Dr. King says in the closing lines of his speech, "The oceans of history are made turbulent by the ever-rising tides of hate. History is cluttered with the wreckage of nations and individuals that pursued this self-defeating path of hate. As Arnold Toynbee says: 'Love is the ultimate force that makes for the saving choice of life and good against the damning choice of death and evil. Therefore the first hope in our inventory must be the hope that love is going to have the last word.'"

So we sit. We chant. We wrap each other's pain in a unity of voices and sing.

Deep in my heart, I do believe, we shall overcome someday.

The greatest threat to crowd control is our individual yearning for something better. Maybe it is in the clouds, but it is definitely in company *with* each other. We are not hungry for the brains of the living—we have our own, thank you very much. We are yearning to connect with others, to be engaged in collective action. The greatest source of our self-defense against the mob mentality of law and order politics is each other. This is not a romantic notion of connection. It is not about connecting as couples or nice, neat households. Not because we are friends or lovers or because we share a common social network, but because we know and share a common knowledge that the personal is political, but the impersonal is powerful. Our greatest liability is thinking we have to go it alone. That we should trust no one. That no one gets us, or our struggle. That we are surrounded by those who will misread and abuse us. No doubt they are. No doubt they will. No doubt they are legion. But they are not the end of our world. Even if they kill us. Chances are they all have their own struggles too. Strength in numbers is not only about meeting the might of the opposition with everything we got. It's about each of us finding strength in ourselves we never knew possible at the side of another we don't have to share blood or fluids with to feel. It is about fellowship within the fray of friction. We might not all feel the same for the same reasons, but we don't have to. We are not mercenaries. We are defending ourselves against the modern threats of mass disposability. We are not just hungry, we are starving. We could become one rather than scramble to defend *our* stuff and *our* families. Together, there are no individual selves to be defended. Together, self-defense is collective transformation.

IT'S NOT ABOUT LOVE AFTER ALL

by Rev. angel Kyodo williams, Sensei

We have witnessed the way in which movements for justice that denounce dominator culture, yet have an underlying commitment to corrupt uses of power, do not really create fundamental changes in our societal structure. When radical activists have not made a core break with dominator thinking (imperialist, white supremacist, capitalist patriarchy), there is no union of theory and practice, and real change is not sustained.... It is precisely because the dictates of dominator culture structure our lives that it is so difficult for love to prevail.

—BELL HOOKS

Without inner change, there can be no outer change, without collective change, no change matters.

—REV. ANGEL KYODO WILLIAMS, SENSEI

I have been mulling over the role of love in movements for well over two decades now. I felt a sense of calling to activist work—ushering in the third wave of feminism and changing minds about the so-called apathetic Generation X. Our cross-country voter registration drive felt significant, and I felt like I was part of something making a difference. Not too much later, after I dropped anchor in a spiritual practice, the conflicting ideas that seemed almost normal became increasingly apparent.

Like many activists, I was alarmed by the destructive behavior of my comrades and colleagues, and confounded by how it could be possible we would ever create the world we wanted to live in if we could not be the change. Although we were young women with good models for kindness toward each other, much of our work was driving against this or that, and to drive so hard and fast required fuel, and that fuel was anger.

VEHICLES TO FREEDOM: WHAT'S YOUR RIDE?

Starting out five hundred to six hundred years before the Common Era, the historic Buddha taught for over fifty years. His teachings naturally evolved over his own lifetime, and he died leaving a significant wealth of discourses. By the fourteenth century, what was referred to simply as the teachings of the Buddha had virtually disappeared from the land of its birth in India. As the teachings found themselves in different countries stretched out over hundreds, then even a thousand years, different aspects were focused on.

FIRST TURNING—HINAYANA, SMALLER VEHICLE
ARHAT IDEAL: CODES OF CONDUCT AND LIBERATION FOR ONE'S SELF

Not long after finding my place as an activist for social justice, I came up against the need for not just reacting to what was happening in the world, which gave me a sense of purpose, but developing a way to look at what was happening, which provided a sense of meaning. I found a second home in cultivating a spiritual life. Though I didn't originally think of it that way, my formal Zen practice and training were teaching me to find a more restful place that I could abide in within myself despite the chaos and calamity that living in an unjust society meant we were constantly surrounded by. It also gave me a way to be in response to sometimes overwhelming situations that could just lead me to a downward spiral of anger and negativity. I didn't know a lot, but I knew that I didn't want to live a life driven by anger and rage. I could see that many activist elders and now my younger counterparts had fallen into that vortex, and it seemed difficult to get out once you were caught there.

THE WAKE-UP WARRIORS

SECOND TURNING—MAHAYANA, GREATER VEHICLE
BODHISATTVA IDEAL: COMPASSION AND LIBERATION FOR THE SAKE OF OTHERS

But the Zen community I eventually became engaged with did not frame its cultivation of peace as a passive practice because we had a set of vows that I took to heart. In fact, the reason I decided to make a home with these particular folks was precisely because, as the Zen Peacemaker Order, they were explicitly committed to social action.

I was captivated by the bodhisattva ideal. The most prominent *Avalokiteshvara* is "he who looks down on" and is embodied as female in Chinese, or "the one who hears the cries of the world." In *bodhisattvas*, I saw Sojourner and Ella, Ambedkar and Malcolm. In their infinite wisdom and boundless compassion, they responded to the cries. Even though liberation is available to them, they hold it off until every person can be awakened, too. What I didn't hear is that I need anger to drive my response.

I lived by this ideal for many years; I extrapolated and built upon the concept of the "awakening warrior," as I'd heard it translated in Tibetan teachings. Strongly influenced by Chö-gyam Trungpa Rinpoche's teachings on the enlightened society of Shambhala, and the qualities of warriorship needed to achieve it, warrior-spirit became a central theme of my work. I advocated for this more balanced approach to fiercely address injustice from a place of empowerment as a warrior—but one that was ultimately committed to peace rather than aggression. This path recognized the clarity and resilience brought about by cultivating one's inner life and recognizing the ego as the ultimate foe to be vanquished. I saw this as a more sustainable path, especially for Black people, whose road to victory in the external landscape would likely be a long one given the deep entrenchment of the forces of oppression set against us.

In response to the events of September 11th, I wrote what became known as the Warrior-Spirit Prayer of Awakening. The verse became an affirmation of how I wanted to be in response to the challenges of the world and eventually became the penultimate call of the practice community I eventually founded.

Warrior-Spirit Prayer of Awakening

योधात्मनः प्रार्थना बोधनस्य

yodhaatmanah praarthanaa bodhanasya

May all beings be granted with the strength, determination and wisdom to extinguish anger and reject violence as a way.

सर्वे मानवाः आप्नुवंतु शक्ति निश्चयं प्रज्ञां च
क्रोधं प्रणष्टुं हिंसां परित्यक्तुं च सदा

sarve maanavaah aapnuvantu shaktim nishchayam pradnyaam cha
krodham pranashtum hinsaam parityaktum cha sadaa

May all suffering cease and may I seek, find, and fully realize the love and compassion that already lives within me and allow them to inspire and permeate my every action.

सर्वबाधाः विरमंतु च मृग्याणि आप्नवानि
पूर्णतः अनुभवानि च प्रेम करुणां च पूर्वमेव
मयि स्थिते च मनुमन्यै ते विश्वसितुं व्याप्तुं
च मम सर्वकर्माणि च

sarvabaadhaah wiramantu cha mrigyaani aapnawaani
poornatah anubhavaani cha prema karunaam cha poorvameva
mayi sthite cha anumanyai te wishvasitum wyaaptum
cha mama sarvakarmaani cha

May I exercise the precious gift of choice and the power to change that which makes me uniquely human and is the only true path to liberation.

योजानि अम्लूयपारतोषकिं वरस्य शक्तिं
परविर्तति्ं च यथा मां करोति अद्वितीयत्वेन
मानवं चास्ति एक: एव मार्ग: म्कुत्यैं च

yojaani amoolya paaritoshikam warasya shaktim
parivartitum cha yathaa maam karoti adwiteeyatwena
maanavam chaasti ekah eva maargah muktyai cha

May I swiftly reach complete, effortless freedom so that my fearless, unhindered action be of benefit to all.

गच्छानि पूर्णस्वात्त्र्यमनायासेन यथा
ममाभयानवरोधकर्माणि सर्वेषां हितं क्ुर्वंत्

gachchhaani poornaswaatantryamanaayaasena yathaa
mamaabhayaanawarodhakarmaani sarveshaam hitam kurwamtu

May I lead the life of a warrior.

मम जीवनं योधस्यास्तु

mama jeevanam yodhasyaastu

BEYOND ALLIES

THIRD TURNING–VAJRAYANA: INDESTRUCTIBLE VEHICLE
LIBERATION IN THIS LIFETIME

As I began to feel as powerful as the bodhisattva was, not only compassion was enough; I wanted also to confront the things that existed in my self that got in the way. I wanted to go to the heart of change by cultivating indestructible qualities.

By this time, I had read bell hooks's earth-shattering book, *All About Love*. I was inspired to take up the investigation of love more rigorously. My experience with Zen—in fact, with most of the expression of the white Western-convert Buddhism I was in contact with—was that, though compassion was an ever-attending partner to wisdom, love was hyphenated into a concept that felt more neutral. Lovingkindness, a common translation of *metta*, promoted good behavior but lacked the fire of fierce love I knew and felt in my colored upbringing. Even the joy that was considered one of the Four Immeasurable Qualities was denatured, and the Zen folks, myself included, seemed to prefer the last Immeasurable Quality, equanimity. I found the warmth of love, if not always the word, expressed in Tibetan teachings, in Advaita, with my yoga tribe. bell's work brought me back to a more explicit naming of and focus on love as a motivating force for change.

FOURTH TURNING—MITRAYANA: FRIENDSHIP VEHICLE
LIBERATION BY COLLECTIVE

My intense interest and eventual certainty about the connection between inner change and social change led me to go beyond studying what made change possible in people and think about how deeply powerful change could be scaled to movements to affect many people—by reaching a critical mass of change-makers who could, on their own terms, cultivate indestructible qualities, but, all working together, could create movements that weren't about a small handful of individuals doing things on behalf of the many but enrolling people in the deep project of their own liberation.

MEETING SUFFERING

The thing about our pain and our suffering is that until it is met and seen for what it is, it doesn't go anywhere. It's like the dark places in your refrigerator, things hidden in little containers that you refuse to open because you don't quite remember when it got there. So instead of opening and facing the smelly containers you find, you ignore them and eventually run into an infestation, an overgrowth of mold and spores and bacteria and things that can kill you, because you didn't want to deal with them when they were just plain stinky.

BE WITH THE SUFFERING

The very first thing the Buddha taught, the First Noble Truth, was that we have to come to terms with the fact that the nature of life is to experience confusion and discomfort. That by the fact of our birth, old age, sickness, and death are in our future, and we are thus inclined to suffer.

In our culture, so much is oriented toward moving away from that experience and finding ways to deaden it, whether that's through addictions to Facebook, television, drugs, or alcohol. You have to figure out:

What place are you not feeling?

What part of you are you rejecting?

What aspect are you not loving?

What truth are you not willing to accept?

In my experience, whatever we're not facing about ourselves is never as bad as the ideas we are referencing ourselves off of. The funny thing is that somehow when we get caught in our stuck ideas about ourselves, we create better images of who we are and we simultaneously believe worse images of who we actually are. So we create fantasies and we believe fiction. Neither of these things abide in truth.

It's easier to leave these parts aside, at least to our conscious mind, than to even begin to consider if we will be able to survive the grief of facing them. It's easier to just claim our progressiveness, to claim our enlightened hearts and spirits or our radicalness and commitment to the struggle—so you can't possibly be racist, or sexist, or transphobic, or think your spirituality is more real, or you're just better—than to actually have your despair show up for you. In truth, we have to integrate our wounds into our understanding of who we are and what we are really capable of so that we can be whole human beings. Only from there can we begin the process of healing the brokenness, the broken-heartedness within ourselves that is then the foundation for beginning to heal that in our larger society.

We cannot have a healed society, we cannot have change, we cannot have justice if we do not reclaim and repair the human spirit. We simply cannot. Imagining anything different is to really have our head buried deeply in the sand of hundreds of years of a culture of domination, colonization, the theft of this land, the theft of a people from their land, and the continued and ongoing theft and appropriation of peoples and cultures on a day-to-day basis that every single one of us is colluding with and participating in consciously and unconsciously.

Learning to be with suffering as an experience is part and parcel of what it means to live, and it radically alters our relationship to all of life and to the suffering of others. If you are invested in alleviating suffering, whether as an activist or change-maker or someone who's committed to life because you hear the cries of the world, it's important to understand that you can't even recognize the suffering of others without fully acknowledging the despair of your own suffering. It turns out that far from dragging you down, one of the most liberating things you can do is to come to terms with the fact that some form of your suffering will always be there. To really be present with that unhooks us from the constant anxiety of trying to make it go away. Paradoxically, once we release the proposition that we are going to get rid of the suffering, then the potential to alleviate the suffering becomes possible.

THE GRAND CENTRAL STATION OF PRESENCE

The most important thing to unpack is what would draw people into this ever-deepening path. What could be both the motivation and the destination?

It seems to me that for people to develop any of the qualities that were important for nurturing people's inner life—their sense of commitment beyond instant gratification, the long-term investment that it takes to dismantle such daunting and interrelated structures of oppression—we had to use a new approach.

We keep trying to approach things from the vehicle of "other," as in what people should do for "the other" and what we end up doing is othering. But when shit hits the fan, we run the other way and create more distance. The question is: how do we allow people to be deeply in touch with themselves, and allow them to become deeply in touch with others?

They have to cultivate their capacity for presence. Presence is Grand Central Station and the place people arrive from wherever they've originally come from—fear, anger, disappointment, anxiety. Through the practice of being present to their situations, to the suffering that they felt as a result, not to mention the power of being seen as others are present with them, they can then travel on to compassion, to courage, to caring, to love.

We don't have to fix people at all. We have to trust the evolutionary draw that is. What pulls you forward is presence. Presence is what motivates people and what you get out of it. As you choose to be more present, you are more present. What does presence allow? It allows us to see ourselves and others. By choosing presence we learn to let go of our own discomfort, and experiencing ourselves in a trusting way allows us to trust others more. As a result, we are drawn deeper.

EVERY BODY HOME

Predatory capitalist greed has deeply ingrained a self-worth confusion into our psyche. We associate our value as human beings with our financial worth. Our relationships are governed by the shadow game of acquisition. We can never have enough. The result is a devastating disconnect to a felt sense of our experience.

Even with meditation, we remain mesmerized by the elusive possibility of one day becoming the elite. We contort our bodies and fling our values into suspension in the air between the seat of our soul and the elusive brass ring. How can the core remain intact if the appendages are hyperextended into the posture of overreach that consumption lust seduces us into?

I introduced embodiment practice to invite people back home to their felt experience. To disrupt the disconnect among head and heart, aligned thought, emotions, and action that a no-longer citizen, but consumer society, fosters. I believe anyone engaged in the practice of liberation must actively discover it in their own being, and having a body-based or somatic practice is a direct way to reclaim connection to their psycho-physical connection to themselves.

THEORY OF A TRANSFORMATIVE SOCIAL CHANGE

Transformative Social Change as applied to efforts and just change was the way in which I tried to speak to, articulate, and concretize something that I knew intuitively. It is a theory of change, so it is living.

In order to not just organize people against a this or that only to fall away again, it seemed important to support people in a recognition of the potential for liberation.

Transformative Social Change applies to what used to be called Liberation Spirituality, but I insist we not limit it to spirituality and look at it as an emergent movement. Agnostics, atheists, or even humanists can go through this process. History is there (Gandhi, King, etc.), but this new iteration is unique in that both Eastern and Western views are being held by an individual, and it's no longer associated around a singular or dominant spiritual, religious tradition or cluster (Abrahamic, Dharmic, etc.) or even of any religion or spiritual tradition at all.

On the one hand, Transformative Social Change is inherently spiritual, but not in the sense of a particular tradition. To call it merely spiritual is arrogant as it suggests that we have a corner on the market of what is spiritual—and by association, what is not. It is naive. Spirituality, by its nature, has a whole expressive range. Transformative Social Change looks specifically at "what is the trajectory?" and "what is the vehicle?" of the desired change.

Spiritual tradition is comfortable with paradox, whereas many political movements are not. But all truth is paradox. What it is to live in a space of transformative change is to engender greater and greater comfort with paradox. So that paradox becomes something that we not only acknowledge but also live more truthfully. We discover that Truth *is* relationship. And relationship *is*.

THE LANGUAGE OF LOVE

The theory of Transformative Social Change was designed to do exactly what bell hooks speaks of, to unite theory and practice, providing an identifiable yet adaptive, concrete yet flexible, rigorous yet permeable path to breaking with dominator culture through direct experience. Through praxis. But having folded behavior, motivation, community, suffering, presence, and embodiment into a theory of a truly transformative change, I was still challenged by a phenomenon I couldn't quite make sense of.

WHERE'S THE LOVE?

My life is full of rich relationships to white people. I have been in community with and traveled among many of them, and know of many more who would fiercely claim they are motivated by love. I'm speaking of my fellow Buddhist teachers and practitioners, tribes of yoga practitioners, even legions of progressive activists who focus on change in "rights" and entitlements but shy away from justice, which would impact the positioning and access to those things that are inalienable to human thriving. Most painfully, they are not sufficiently motivated by their sense of love to courageously confront capitalism and its white knight of supremacy as a systemic purveyor of mass suffering. Neither are they willing to see their own belief in the superiority of whiteness play out in everyday interactions as unconscious bias, micro-aggressions, and a tendency to exert control over cultural norms and space. They find a never-ending litany of excuses to maintain power over rather than power with—to dominate.

They are not experiencing love as an earthy, grounding power to be wielded for justice, sometimes with attending fire that burns through whatever may obscure truth, as I believed would be most natural. Rather, they hold it as a more air-like element, one they are certain of the need for, the one that is sustained by and benefits from breathing in deeply, but that is an ultimately private affair expressed only on the interpersonal realm. This is the first window into solving my dilemma: no one wants to be told they do not love, nor, short of being a sociopath, would it be accurate.

It wouldn't be fair of me to say that they were not committed to love, and yet, they are not activated into responding to the obvious, pressing injustices of society.

What dawned on me is that not only has white supremacy robbed red, Black, brown, and yellow people of the spirit-given human right to life and liberty, it has also so thoroughly programmed and policed white people as to who and how they could love—determining entire groups of people unworthy—that the entirety of our descended culture suffers from a severely atrophied relationship to the most animating, enlivening, equalizing force gifted to the human experience.

The opposite of love is not hate, it's indifference.
—ELIE WIESEL

How else could the imaginably decent, moral, ordinary white people stand to live in proximity, much less partake, in open-market slavery? Generations of people allowed their children to witness the sale and degradation of other human bodies. This most unnatural of arrangements, executed for nothing more aspirational than the privilege of financial gain, required the compulsion toward compassion for other beings to be systematically uprooted and replaced with widespread indifference. This has continued into post-slavery lynching, Jim Crow denial of legal entitlements, systematic mass incarceration, prison-to-school pipelines, and so on. All of this has occurred while white folks gained from the resulting wealth, presumption of entitlement to fare better than colored people, and, most insidiously, a belief that meritocracy has been at work all along, shielding them behind a cloak of ignorance and innocence while they cash their spoils at the bank.

For generation upon generation, white America has traded its humanity for privilege.

The tax, though, has been on love, which peace pays the premium for. In personal, interpersonal, and social spheres, our worlds become smaller, potential thwarted, possibility more limited when the creative force of love is reigned in.

Even our great social currency of language is anemic when it comes to expression of love. Sanskrit, the language of dharmic religions, has ninety-six words for love. Persian, eighty. It has often been shared that Greek, which we borrow from, has six words that can help us make distinctions: agape, eros, ludus, philautia, philia, and pragma; but most of us cannot recall them, much less have an active understanding and practice. The politics of respectability and the hidden rules of politeness that silently govern white belonging to "proper society" demand that love remain personal. The further the love is from some norm, the more behind closed doors, in the closet, relegated to corners of guilt, laden with shame it must be. The result of having "privatized" love is we are not comfortable with its raw, unabashed, unapologetic, unmitigated expression. Love for one another, especially across lines of difference, has been taboo for the overwhelming part of our national lives.

The answer to my inquiry about the apparent lack of love manifesting on behalf of justice seems clear: People don't know how to apply love in the great sphere of society.

THE MEASURE OF JUSTICE

Never forget that justice is what love looks like in public.

—Cornel West

The only thing white people have that Black people need, or should want, is power—and no one holds power forever.... And I repeat: The price of the liberation of the white people is the liberation of the Blacks—the total liberation, in the cities, in the towns, before the law, and in the mind.

—James Baldwin, *The Fire Next Time*

SECTION III:

THE CONVERSATIONS

GUESS WHO'S COMING TO DINNER: HISTORY OF THIS PROJECT

Radical Dharma emerged from kindred wisdom traditions and prophetic voices passed on generation after generation from all the peoples of the four directions. It emerges now as a collaborative response to a collective call from the American Buddhist community for new ways to talk about the presence of white supremacy in our centers, practices, and lives. The call initially came in late summer of 2014 when Lama Rod and Rev. angel were asked by their colleagues at *Buddhadharma* magazine to talk about their practice of radical dharma. The ensuing dialogue gave them a chance to collaborate for the first time and begin to practice what they found was a level of vulnerability and love between two teachers of color—voices that are rarely heard in this conversation together.

This has been a process Rev. angel and Lama Rod have found to be a privilege, an honor, but also a challenge. "As teachers sometimes people don't allow us to struggle and to connect to some of these things we're all still working out," they have said. To sit as Buddha dharma siblings and friends and comrades and co-conspirators is the beginning of the practice of collective liberation. It is modeling what radical dharma practice can look like in our *sanghas* and our communities—the kind of courage, openness, and camaraderie needed for talking about race and the woundedness that many of us experience in the world and in our spiritual communities.

Radical Dharma began as a conversation on race, love, and

liberation motivated in part by the mass mobilizations against the state-sanctioned killing of Michael Brown in Ferguson, Missouri. The dialogue between Rev. angel and Lama Rod struck a chord within the Buddhist community. A video of the conversation was released online the very day the country was reeling from the no-indictment verdict in the case of Michael Brown. The Eric Garner decision shortly followed. By Buddhist standards, the video went "viral." So Lama Rod and Rev. angel got to talking about the uniqueness of where their own experiences called them to—to speak in terms of the dharma. Their own histories and own experiences as dharma practitioners and teachers differ and are both distinct from many of those of the teachers we have seen for the first five decades of Buddhism in America.

The impetus to turn this initial conversation into a book was very much inspired by the Black oral tradition. And so Cornel West's and bell hooks's *Breaking Bread* immediately came to mind as a model. Published in 1991, *Breaking Bread* is what has been called a "talking book." It was a pivotal book and groundbreaking at the time. It examined the diversity of perspectives that make up the prophetic tradition; in so doing it centered two Black intellectuals. At the time it was not an expected discourse. The book followed a series of conversations recorded between them, as well as some essays. So we thought, "Wouldn't it be powerful to have something like that for Buddhism?" To make it as organic as possible, we thought, "Well, we'll just go have the conversations." We ultimately chose four venues where one or more of us was already rooted: Atlanta, New York, Boston, and Berkeley. We wanted to bring the history and legacy of the Black prophetic voice into the American Buddhist community and reframe this call for conversation about race, love, and liberation as part of one many folks of color have been having with each other for decades.

We strongly believe that now is the time for us to begin having this conversation about the responsibility of the Buddhist community to confront white supremacy in our *sanghas* and in our communities. We recognized that this particular moment calls for a particular kind of conversation about and attention to what has been missing from our dharma practice—an integration of the ways we are present or not to the issues of race, love, and liberation that shape our collective awakening.

We went on the road and visited various kinds of communities across the country. In Atlanta we visited with Shambhala Meditation Center and Charis Books. In New York, it was Brooklyn Zen Center. In Boston, we met at Harvard Divinity School, which Lama Rod attends. And in Berkeley, we hosted the conversation at the Center for Transformative Change, which was founded by Rev. angel.

About the journey, Lama Rod said, "I don't see our time together as dialogue; I see it as sharing—as loving one another. I see it as making love."

In each venue the participants represented a spectrum of ethnic and racial backgrounds, ages, and relationships to the dharma including folks who had a *sangha* and a practice to those with a practice and no *sangha* to those for whom formal dharma practice was completely new.

THE SHAMBHALA CENTER AND CHARIS BOOKS, ATLANTA, GA

Atlanta was perhaps a very unlikely first site of Radical Dharma. Lama Rod grew up outside of Atlanta and is familiar with the area. With Lama Rod's closest friend Jamie Fergerson working with Jasmine, we were able to secure two venues. The first was at the Shambhala Meditation Center on Saturday, March 21, 2015. Located in the Decatur area of Atlanta, the center is a cluster of buildings with a main building housing the large beautiful meditation hall arranged in the style that the tradition's founder, Chögyam Trungpa Rinpoche, most appreciated. The next day, Sunday, March 22, the second Radical Dharma dialogue was hosted by Charis Books located in the Atlanta neighborhood of Little Five Points, famous for its alternative culture scene. Charis Books itself is the oldest feminist bookstore in the South.

The dialogues were the first time Rev. angel and Lama Rod sat together as formal teachers and were the first time Lama Rod met Jasmine. Participants at both events were eager to talk about the challenges of inclusivity and racism in their *sanghas*. What was also special at Charis was the presence of Professor Jan Willis, who is not only one of the first Black female Buddhist scholars but an important scholar in American Buddhism.

BROOKLYN ZEN CENTER, BROOKLYN, NY

The Brooklyn Zen Center (BZC) is located in the Gowanus section of Brooklyn. It is an urban center with a sense of serious practice happening right within a busy, trendy, and ever-gentrifying neighborhood. BZC practices in the tradition of Soto Zen Buddhism and seeks to offer practice that is in tune to the diverse and demanding lives of practitioners. The center can easily be called contemporary—not a contemporary that discards tradition but a contemporary that embraces tradition and moves boldly forward into the present, integrating what is important for practitioners now with what practitioners need from tradition. The center seems to be located in an older remodeled factory building. The meditation takes place in a large warm room with wood-paneled floors and walls made of exposed brick painted in white as well as drywall in white. New York is where Rev. angel grew up while Jasmine moved to the area as a teenager. The center is a teaching home for Rev. angel in New York. On Saturday, April 18, 2015, the third Radical Dharma dialogue between Rev. angel and Lama Rod was facilitated by Jasmine. It was one of the largest gatherings for Radical Dharma. Participants were diverse and mostly not affiliated with the center. The conversation was lively and characterized by several white participants naming their own struggle with whiteness.

HARVARD DIVINITY SCHOOL, CAMBRIDGE, MA

The Braun Room in Andover Hall at Harvard Divinity School is a symbol of academia. With its conservative décor of wood-paneled walls, tall windows, portraits of several notable professors and deans (mostly white), a large fireplace, and one wall of shelves covered with books, it was perhaps an unlikely venue for a Radical Dharma dialogue. However, one of the tenets of Radical Dharma is to take the conversation into spaces that need the conversation and especially into spaces that represent a kind of academic elitism that is also an expression of traditional white supremacy. The space is used for community gatherings and special events, including talks by visiting lecturers or visits by notable figures such as His Holiness the 17th Gyalwang Karmapa. Lama Rod is a student there in the Master of Divinity program. On Thursday April 30, 2015, it was the site of the fourth Radical Dharma talk with Rev. angel and Lama Rod, facilitated by Erika Carlsen, one of Lama Rod's colleagues at Harvard Divinity School, who stepped in for Jasmine. Close to one hundred people were in attendance, bringing with them what seemed to be more of an intellectual approach to the dialogue of a liberatory Dharma.

CENTER FOR TRANSFORMATIVE CHANGE, BERKELEY, CA

On Wednesday, June 17, 2015, a young white man gunned down nine Black church folk at Emanuel African Methodist Episcopal (AME) Church in Charleston, South Carolina. On Friday, June 19, we gathered for the fifth Radical Dharma talk at Rev. angel's center, the Center for Transformative Change, in Berkeley, California. The night was charged, for it was not only two days after the massacre, but also June 19, a day celebrated in communities across the country as Juneteenth, the day in 1865 that the last slaveholding state, Texas, received word that the war was over and that President Lincoln had emancipated slaves two years prior. We assembled in the small practice hall located on a separate structure in the back of the center and nestled in a small Japanese-style garden. The moderate Bay Area summer offered a kind of lightness that helped in holding our collective mourning and hurt. This talk was different. Our realities of being marginalized and oppressed bodies experiencing psychophysical trauma was upfront and heavy that night. We began the evening with a formal memorial ritual evoking the names of the victims while remembering the words of Dr. King and evoking the transcendental wisdom of the Heart Sutra. More than any other gathering, we needed to evoke liberation.

FLOW OF THE EVENING

Each evening began with introductions and a dialogue between Rev. angel and Lama Rod that went on from thirty-five to forty-five minutes to whet everyone's palette and seed the conversation. We then opened up the dialogue to the larger community and really allowed ourselves to have ample opportunity for interaction with what was present for the community.

While there were no hard rules for engaging in the community conversation, there were some key guidelines the teachers offered at each convening. The first was an invitation from Rev. angel that we leave niceness aside. She made a careful distinction between what it means to be kind to each other, rather than trying to be nice. Rev. angel reminded us that

> *"this is a conversation that is long overdue, and we should take the opportunity of us being in the room together, but you're also welcome to challenge us. Please don't regard the fact that we are teachers as meaning that we can't be challenged. And we give good push-back. So please do just bring your full heart and your full voice, and I trust that your being here means that you are rooted in love, and that's what you can bring to this conversation."*

A second guideline for holding this conversation in a good way came from Lama Rod, who echoed the importance of being kind but also invited us into being messy, because we create much more damage in our communities and our relationships when we are always editing everything. Lama Rod placed this in the context of the current culture of silences and hesitations to speak our truths regarding race, love, and liberation, both in our dharma communities and in our everyday lives.

"I think so many people are afraid to actually express how they feel because it's so uncomfortable. A lot of my work is around really working with the wounded, the trauma in people, bringing these really difficult things into the practice. And it's really not comfortable as Rev. angel said. I want people to have a sense of agency, and I need people to feel as though they're a part of the transformation. Not just sitting there and trying to get something from me."

We began by thinking together about what truths this conversation of race, love, and liberation bring up for us. We asked what came up for the community in their own experience, in their own practice, in their own centers. What we heard was the radical expression of dharma. It brought truth into the room through their questions, their curiosities, their frustrations and wonderings. We asked folks to reflect upon how they understand folks of color to be central to our practice. What we wanted to do was generate a new protocol of truth-telling in regard to race, love, and liberation.

MEAL GATHA[4]

We express our gratitude for this food that comes to us from the lives of plants and animals, from the light and warmth of the sun, the earth's fertile soil, the heavenly rain, the labor of farmers, the work of transportation and the services of merchants.

Considering where this food has come from and the many labors that have brought it to us, we resolve to strengthen our body, to awaken our mind and to enrich our spirit.

Reflecting on all those who are in need of nourishment, we eat this food.

Resolving to think good thoughts and to do good deeds, we eat this food.

Committing to serve all those who strive to break their addictions and transform their delusions, we eat this food.

Vowing to attain our Way, we eat this food.

May we exist in muddy water with purity like a lotus, thus we eat this food.

DINNER DIALOGUE

REV. ANGEL: When I was twenty-two, I would go and visit the Buddhist corner. It was sort of strange because as a queer person I was never in the closet, but I was a closet Buddhist!

---

[4] *Meal Verse* by Bernie Glassman Roshi, cofounder of the Zen Peacemaker Order. Based on the traditional Soto Zen Meal Gatha. *Gatha* is Sanskrit for "a short verse."

It felt odd to be a person manifesting in this body looking at that path. But it called me enough to go and visit a dharma center in the village in Manhattan. There was a lesbian woman teacher there, so that made it easy. This is often how we find church, right? In no time at all, though, I realized I was a little bit different. Not just by age, which was striking—at least ten to twenty years' difference between myself and nearly everyone else. I also stood out because of my color. There is no dearth of people of color in Manhattan, so at first I thought I was just coming on the wrong night. You know how that is—a "colored folks night" or something like that…. But I tried all the nights and it was the same. I even tried coming early in the morning. I didn't think it was really true: the folks of color were really going to be there, but they weren't.

And yet there was nothing after a few weeks that the people there were saying that seemed so strange or foreign-tongued that folks that I knew and loved couldn't get it. In fact, that *sangha* was profoundly helpful. The first thing that they do often at centers is get you to have some type of position. So they are like: "Oh, angel, you're here again. Would you like to do the drum tonight?" I thought, "Oh, OK …"

LAMA ROD: Repeat the rhythm.

REV. ANGEL: Yes, "Give the Black folks the drum." And I was all kind of offended until I realized that they always give people the drum first. And frankly, not everyone was given the drum, and they preferred to wait for me to do the rhythm. I felt the striking sense like I was different and that I was alone in that difference. And I so unfolded my life within Buddhist practice with the profound sense of aloneness and yet a simultaneous sense of having found home.

LAMA ROD: That echoes my experience as well. I came into dharma after coming out of a really severe period of clinical depression, and I was taught meditation to work with that condition. It was the most successful of the strategies I'd tried, and I actually emerged from that experience going back to church and singing in the choir. I found Jesus again, but he wasn't necessarily talking to me. And so I began to turn my attention to Buddhism, partially because my housemates were practicing it. And so it was like my tradition was picked for me, and I entered into that practice understanding that this is exactly what I was supposed to be doing in this life. And this is an experience many people don't have. It was like I had made these choices before. I had written the script and now in this particular location I was just playing my rightful role.

My teacher at the time gave me a picture of her two teachers, two, very attractive men, one older and one younger. They looked like father and son, and I was like, wow. This must be the lineage of beautiful people. *That's where I belonged!*

REV. ANGEL: Does anyone know anything about the teachings of attachment? [Laughter]

LAMA ROD: You call it attachment. I call it blessings. I call it motivation. I call it excitement. I was like, where do I sign? Eventually, I learned that this taller young man was named Karmapa and the shorter older man was Tai Situ Rinpoche, who was one of the head lamas in my tradition. I felt pulled toward these teachers, and sometimes we need a hook. It's a karmic hook, and I used it to draw and invite myself into this profound relationship.

At the same time, I was also the only Black person going through this process. From the outset Rinpoche said, "I don't see race. Do you understand?" I was like, "Yes," because what he was really saying with that statement was, "I know that you're going to start running some games with me about how you deserve more because you're the only one. But you have to do exactly what everyone else has to do because that is what will make your experience meaningful." I understood that at the moment.

REV. ANGEL: Were you planning on running some games?

LAMA ROD: Well, I was used to it. I'm used to being the only one. You get to do certain things because you need to represent a group: "Oh, we need some color here." Maybe you'll get in in the pictures and end up on the website! There is a tendency to use brown people to make statements. I've had to develop self-awareness of when I'm being used in that way.

REV. ANGEL: The relationship between race and privilege is complex. Definitely colored folks have privilege that sometimes gets bestowed upon them exactly because of their race. And yet we're told, "You're not going to be treated special." It's an ongoing dialectic that rarely offers liberation. I remember once attending a retreat with fifty other people, forty-seven of whom were white. One woman looked at me and asked, "Do you know that they're going to have a *Martin Luther King* Day retreat here?" She put great emphasis on "Martin Luther King." The color of my skin was both something to be called out and yet something to be utterly undealt with.

LAMA ROD: She was trying to make you feel special and welcomed into the space.

REV. ANGEL: I'm sure she was. I was not feeling welcome, that's for sure. The real question remains: How can we address the barriers for people like me when the predominant culture cannot acknowledge its privilege? We are born into a particular body, and this can be a great source of pain, depending on how society views the identity [associated with it]. And yet, communities in power pretend the difference, and the pain, is not there, which causes the individuals in that skin to question our value.

LAMA ROD: So those who are being devalued—whether it's because of race, gender, economics, sexuality—are the ones forced to articulate that experience of being devalued, in essence reflecting that truth back to those who have the privilege of doing the devaluing?

REV. ANGEL: Right. And there is woundedness all along this line. And there are strange, relative roles within power. I've had to realize I have privilege around being fairer and having Eurocentric-type hair!

LAMA ROD: Good hair.

REV. ANGEL: Yes, good hair. Most Black communities call it good hair. I had curly hair and spoke the King's English, as I like to say. I was told I was articulate so often, as if it were unusual. So I'm moving through the world with a different set of privileges than my darker brown-skinned, kinky-haired brothers and sisters are. I unconsciously kept this power dynamic in place, partially because I got benefits from being special. We are all caught in this crazy web of dysfunction and disconnect as a result of where we sit along the spectrum of color and other forms of marginalization. It's an important entryway into the potential for healing when we start to recognize we are all participating unless we're interrupting. The momentum of the dysfunction of how privilege operates in this society is such that if we're not interrupting, we're actually participating in it.

RADICAL DHARMA: RACE

*the great fraud of the construct of whiteness is that it has
coerced and convinced most white folks to no longer see their
own oppression: by men over women, by straights over LGBT,
by hetero fathers over their sons in arbitrating their masculinity,
by capitalist values of personal acquisition over the personal
freedom of one's soul. white folks have been duped to trade
their humanity for their privilege. the most insidious lie is that
racism is a Black problem or colored folks problem. white folks
wake up: not only oppressed people are complicit in oppression.
it's your problem, too.*

—Rev. angel Kyodo williams, Sensei, December 2014
(Facebook post)

BUILDING THE COMMUNITY

MALE SPEAKER: I've seen other people that actually come
on Tuesday nights that are people of color.

FEMALE SPEAKER: What I'm talking about is people coming to commit to building the community, not just coming
now and then.

FEMALE SPEAKER: We have people of color who come on
Tuesday nights, but you don't see them come back consistently.
They don't feel like they're a part of this system.

Oftentimes, people of color don't see anybody at the door—
they don't see anybody sitting up there on the mat who looks
like them.

[As a person of color], people come to me and ask me questions about little things that they wouldn't dare come and ask a white person.

REV. ANGEL: Well, it's pure survival. We have been attuned to how to survive the experience of a racist society. Those kinds of subtle things that may not seem like a big deal, "I'm brown, so I'm going to find folks that look like me," are actually survival skills that people of color learn and have to utilize every day. As human beings, we look around and we say, "What works? What's safe?" because too many white spaces turn out to not be safe.

I think that will change once communities are having more conscious conversations about the realities that people are facing and experiencing and not merely trying to change the decoration in the room, because that is insufficient.

FEMALE SPEAKER: Well, this is what I had hoped would happen tonight. I'm hoping that people of color will come in and be inspired to have some thoughts that they can share with the community.

JASMINE: How do we navigate the reality of race specifically in this room—a predominantly white room—as we talk about race in this country? What is the work of white folks? What is the work of people of color? What is our work together? How do we get to a place where we can acknowledge our role in the change we seek, with love but also with clarity?

REV. ANGEL: I think the history of this country has not been honestly spoken, and many people of all races don't know the true history. Because of this, we have a lot of disease in this country, one of which is white supremacy, as well as the ignorance of the benefits of being Caucasian in America.

With many illnesses, if we don't take the scab off and let the pus come out, we can't heal. So I'm happy to be a part of this conversation with a mixed [group] of people, because I don't think a lot of people realize that it's a disease. Some people still say they don't see color, which isn't realistic. Being a Black woman in America, I'm very conscious that I can't express myself as freely as someone who might not look like me or be the same gender that I am.

If we don't look at this disease honestly, we're not going to be able to heal.

Zen tradition doesn't have a centralized structure, but they have power structures. Marginalized people are largely challenged by the power structures. Of course, once you're deeply inside, you may know that there's ways to reorganize your own mind in relationship to that power, but you have to get inside, which is why we see the experience of people coming and leaving. I have the benefit of being invited to different communities. And all white-dominated communities have slightly different permutations of the same thing.

Zen is single teachers. Once the teachers get to be teachers, they get to do anything they want, which is the only reason I can exist and be of use at all. It happens to be built into Zen that now that I'm a teacher they can't say anything really to me.

On the other hand, in non-decentralized structures, teachers of color are threatened with their participation and existence. It's subtle, but they're not as vocal. It's not because they don't think the same thing I do. I'm having the same conversations with them, but the structures that exist and the way the power is disables their voices. That creates a ripple effect. People of color that come go, "OK, this is great. But every time I look up there, once again, I'm being told that the only people that can tell me something about myself and help me to learn and understand myself is someone that has no shared conditional experience with me."

Human beings are about communication, so there's a communication in the power structures themselves. So who's sitting here says something. All my life, this is never who was going to be sitting up here. That meant that I had to, as you said, weather it—stick it out. As the demographic changes and people are more empowered in their own lives and finding power in their own lives, they're more and more unwilling to stick it out.

So as we have more people that are ready and open to different teachings outside of the traditional, conventional religions that they grew up with, they're simultaneously politicized in such a way that they're not willing to subject themselves to what many of us subjected ourselves to for a long time. They've had enough.

BEYOND "A STARBUCKS *SANGHA*"

JASMINE: In the classroom, I often have to remind my students that racism is in the air we breathe. There's no getting out of being implicated by it. We're all affected. Acknowledging it is part of what we can do to fight it.

REV. ANGEL: I have this theory that racism is required in order to keep capitalism in place. There is the form of capitalism that we have—and I'm not mad at trade and exchange and barter and all of that—but cancerous capitalism, hyper-capitalism, parasitic capitalism requires racism in order to keep it in place. It requires a division of peoples so that we can have the people that consume, the people that are producing what is consumed, and, frankly, the people that are consumed.

Not only is racism in our society at large, but it's actually in many ways the format that we are presenting our spiritual offerings in. That channel, that vehicle, that lens of competition in a Starbucks *sangha* means, in many ways, that we have also then taken up the same ways of keeping that in place and making sure that we compete well. We can't compete well if we have a white upper-middle-class *sangha* and they start letting brown and Black and queer people in. We won't compete as well on the level of comfort as the *sangha* that's down the block that looks healthy and white.

FEMALE SPEAKER: I grew up in Utah in a white suburb, mostly surrounded by white people. And that is the social group in which I've always felt the most comfortable because that's what I knew. I've lived all over the country and related to people in different ways, and obviously there's assumptions made based on how I look. There's always been this feeling of longing to fit in, in one group or another.

In that process, there are these moments where you learn what not to say, and how not to be. It feels like all of those moments start to pile on you like a solid lead vest. And you carry that with you. And the process of taking off this really heavy lead vest feels like such an effort. There's also some sort of comfort in that vest, because you've learned how to wear it.

Those moments often are very pregnant. There's a realization of, "How should I be?" And the vest is on, so sometimes I'll just keep wearing that. I'm really curious about that space when there's maybe an opportunity to act or say or voice whatever's really resonating for you.

REV. ANGEL: At some point you said, "Based on how I look." Would you say what that means to you?

FEMALE SPEAKER: Sure. I'm a fair-skinned Black girl. And I've always identified as a Black person even though I'm half-white. I think that there can be these uncomfortable situations where people come up to me and approach me like I'm a sister, you know? And I don't really know how to be in that space. I'm trying to hang with that, but it doesn't feel real because it's not my background. Then there's also hanging out in white communities and people wanting to have these race discussions. I want to be there and hear this, but it's so uncomfortable and unfamiliar.

REV. ANGEL: Thank you for sharing that. I think it's really important that we recognize how complex our realities are, and that we don't share a monolithic Blackness, and that there's no monolithic whiteness, actually. That's part of what the racialization of our society has done, created this place in which we can't really be who we are. So it's difficult for you to just be who you are because there's a whole bunch of assumptions that are foisted on that body and that color.

That's a significant challenge, for colored people and for white people. How ridiculous. Like, you're just white. Like, you don't come from someplace. That is just kind of crazy, right? People have been divorced from their heritage and their complexity and a real connection to what it is that makes up who you are.

I think that's where liberation lies, in those pregnant moments where you have the habit, but if you can see through it, you have this truth. If you don't see it, you can't work with what you don't see. But because you are recognizing the pregnancy of the moment, that means that there's an opportunity to just pull back one little layer of that lead vest. How it will feel is something that only you will know when you actually peel that layer back and see what it's like to be a little more lightened of the burden of carrying other people's projections of you, and not simply being yourself both to the Black folks that want you to be their sister and to the white folks that want you to have all the answers about race.

LAMA ROD: Absolutely. We're born into a situation that's not of our choosing, and there's a condition that comes with that. Awareness is the tool that we're using to look at that and to interrogate. So it's not just my problem. I have work to do, but we all have work to do. My work has been to look at the ways in which I feel like I've never been good enough, to look at the ways in which I feel that I don't deserve something or [at the ways] that it's OK for certain things to happen to me. For other people, perhaps, the work is feeling as if they do have a right to do certain things, to say certain things.

REV. ANGEL: Can you be explicit when you say "other people"?

LAMA ROD: This is across the board, so people with certain power. So you're talking about white folks being born into this kind of conditioning where [their whiteness is] so unconscious to an extent, that there are many cases where they feel like they have a right to say/do certain things, to think certain ways without ever thinking that it's particularly wrong. We see the same thing with gender, sexuality, classes. And for many of us there are boundaries constantly being crossed, and that leads to significant wounding and trauma.

That's the pain, the suffering, the rage, the despair. There's a reality of that that has to be addressed through the work of liberation and healing.

On the other end for white folks, there's still a lot of healing that has to happen. It's a different kind of healing. I think it requires different spaces for that to happen and it's not the oppressed's role to do that work on behalf of the oppressor. We can mirror certain aspects, but the work has to be done by individuals within their groups. Going back to race—there's significant racially induced trauma that we're all struggling to give voice to.

REV. ANGEL: But I mostly hear that people of color have that trauma.

LAMA ROD: I said that we *all* have that trauma. We have different kinds of trauma, but it's still trauma.

FEMALE SPEAKER: I want to say how deeply grateful I am for this conversation and your teaching. How can I focus on racial justice and still address other forms of oppression, some of which interact largely with white supremacy and several of which don't? Specifically, as a disabled person who also faces discrimination on the basis of gender expression and being queer, I really struggle with that. How do I center race fighting white supremacy while still being able to have a love practice extended to myself and to those communities who do, and who don't, experience the breadth of white supremacy and experience intense ableism?

TWO-SPIRITED SPEAKER: I would like to respond. I just finished a six-month training called Untraining White Liberal Racism held here in Berkeley. It happens in three phases, each one is six months long.

A person who looks like myself—sixty-four years old, two-spirited, European American—is generally taken at first glance to be reliable and dependable. I've really begun to notice very closely all the little micro-aggressions against people of color that happen through speech, through behavior, through exclusion, through the general intercourse of social life, and so I like the idea of addressing these in the moment. That's where the change begins to happen and not in the grand scheme of wanting to do something.

When we chanted the speech by Dr. King tonight, I heard

echoes of what Pope Francis advised us to do: changing human behavior and transforming on an individual level.

REV. ANGEL: I feel like white folks actually, contrary to what we've been saying, actually cannot be their full selves as well. And I feel like men can't actually be their full selves when they are trying to navigate, "How do I work with the fact that there's now this marginalized person in the room, and we haven't had any conversation about this? I haven't addressed my suffering about this, and I just don't know what to do. So I need to make you invisible because to make you invisible allows me to be visible again, which is what whiteness and patriarchy essentially do for people. It allows people to be invisible."

LAMA ROD: In person.

REV. ANGEL: I want to ask the audience how many people feel like they get an opportunity to be in spaces where they feel like the suffering that is induced and caused by white folks is actually OK to express? That's fairly few. How many people think it's important for that to be expressed?

FEMALE SPEAKER: Can you repeat your question?

REV. ANGEL: Yes. So whiteness does something in America, right? There are lots of dynamics that spring forth as a result of how that has been constructed in this country and how it continues to play out 450 years later on a daily basis. So what plays out induces suffering. It's the cause of suffering, which includes the suffering of people in relationship to each other. Suffering that they themselves initiate; suffering that they are recipients of.

The human being that sits inside a racialized identity by nature of the society that we're in—there's a person in there that is pre-all of those identities. And yet there's always something that's operating outside of that. That's why I say it's induced by whiteness just like I have forms of experiencing suffering that has been induced by my being seen as a woman, being seen as a person of color. So it's induced by it, rather than inherent to it.

And I mean to say something else about that, because the problem is not whiteness or Blackness. The problem is the way in which we relate to those identities. It isn't inherently a problem to be white. The problem is that we have a whole way of relating to that identity that is the suffering itself, which I think is one of the things that dharma has an awfully good lens on. It's not inherently a problem that I'm *anything*, but the way that I relate to that often as a result of a collective social identity and social way of relating to it—that's actually where the problem lies.

There's nothing wrong with any of us. And there's nothing wrong with any of *who* we are or *who* we were born as and what skin and what gender and what parts we have. That's why I want to keep pointing out that there's a construct happening. Just like ego is a construct. It's something that's out there. And then we have all of these challenges and heaps of suffering that are induced by how we relate to that ego, or that socially induced "identity"—that projection of ourselves.

MALE SPEAKER: Thank you. I'm a racist. And I mean that seriously. I was born into the racist air and water. I'm a recovering racist, and I was also married to a Black woman for twenty years. She passed two years ago, and she opened my eyes and my heart to so many things, including her pain, including my pain as a white man. I'm a member and a teacher of New York Insight [Meditation Center] in Chelsea. We have a number of initiatives bringing people of all backgrounds and all cultures into the *sangha*.

Last month we had an all-day retreat called the "Duty of White Privilege." It was very intense, very challenging, and at times, loving. Six hours together, but it was only white people so that we could provide a secure place for folks to start opening up about their pain.

Someone expressed it as walking on a land-mine field, one slip and they'll be considered racist. In six hours we couldn't even get below the surface to talk about feelings of guilt, feelings of anger toward people of color, feelings of resentment—all the mushy, uncomfortable feelings that are there.

We're now grappling with what do we do next with this. How do we take these initiatives? We have a people of color *sangha*. Last year we had an eight-week beloved-community course where twenty people, again of all backgrounds, come together trying to understand the pain of others, and the pain of self using the tools of the dharma. It's an ongoing, messy, awkward, start-and-stop, and real process. I just want to commend everybody here for partaking in this. Thank you so much for our teachers in organizing this.

FEMALE SPEAKER: I've been a community organizer in the Latino community for a couple years. I spend every day of my life being, a lot of times, the only white person in a group of people of color who are always working for a lot of different issues.

[I'm] trying to understand my place in the organization that I've been working with for a long time. Where are these spaces for the conversations to happen? I get to a place and I'm aware of who's in the room and how I'm making myself disappear in some ways, how in photos I stand behind the sign. What do I do with that?

MALE SPEAKER: I wanted to speak on being an African-American man in America. I grew up here. A lot of my peers who are African American are confronted with hatred and abuse and negativity every day. And yet the goal is to walk with compassion. It's the practice to walk with mindfulness and be aware. And yet you must simultaneously hold the consistent awareness that you may be attacked today.

For the most part, I don't feel hatred toward other people based on race, and I don't discriminate based on race. I look at everyone from open eyes, but I can definitely say that sometimes I just have to disconnect because it can be so trying.

LAMA ROD: This is love, you know? I want to create this message of Black men and women talking to each other and not trying to exert power over one another, not trying to dominate. But just having a conversation and working through the ways in which we've been told to relate to each other and interrogating that resistance and making a choice to love. To love through communicating, through compassion, kindness, and patience.

We hope to work this out in our conversations with one another. I really appreciate you all being here. I encourage you not necessarily to think about being an ally but about getting to the frontlines of your struggle and not just stepping back and saying, "I can't get in the way of marginalized people." Go to your frontlines and be there. That's what's going to make me happy. Don't get behind me.

REV. ANGEL: In this context a conversation about race is critical because the teacher cannot otherwise relate, or is not relating, to where it is we are located. Ultimately, we're not our race and we're not our gender, and we're not all of our external conditions and projections. Our day-to-day experience is colored by that in just the same way that teachers recognize the fact of people's emotions. We also have to acknowledge the fact of the things that are contributing to people's conditioning. If race is not contributing to our conditioning, what is in this country?

If race is not contributing to our conditioning on a daily basis—out the womb, for generations, even before we ourselves got here—then nothing is contributing to our conditioning. And so it feels like such a loss that in a powerful tradition that has the capacity and language for being able to really navigate this mythic, yet real, stratification, this both made-up and felt categorization, then the conversation goes uninitiated. Race is the ultimate delusion in that it both does and does not exist in reality. Somebody went on around and decided to come up with something so that they could sell folks, that they could be "better" than other people, and yet, because of the paradigm, because of the system and structures, the impact of that creation, of that projection, this is felt and experienced as suffering—not only by the people who are on the shit end of the stick but also by the people that are, often unbeknownst to them, continuing to carry that stick.

We're all suffering as a result of not race itself, but our unwillingness to address and be conscious about race and its impacts, how it has been constructed, how it's functioning in our communities, in our traditions, how it is obscuring our teachings and how it is affecting the teachings [people] will interpret and what they will not. What they will share, and what they will not. What they will focus on, and what they will not. Which iconography will be acknowledged, how we interpret that iconography, and what will get left to the side.

LAMA ROD: I think you bring up something important, which is that it's not race itself that's the problem; it's the relationship to it.

Dharma helps us develop a relationship to the nature of

the thing itself. So when people and communities are saying "We're all ultimately the same; there's no such thing as race," ultimately, of course, that's truth, and you want to thank them for their dharma teaching. We all need to be reminded of that, but then we have to bring our focus back to the way in which we still relate to one another as if race and skin color has this inherent meaning. We're creating the meaning, as Rev. angel was just pointing out; we're creating this. And our conversation has to come back to the ways in which we create meaning and deconstruct that through our practices, through our tools of dialogue and critical awareness.

REV. ANGEL: There's also the meaning that was created for us, though, right? The inherited meaning that, without interrogation, we're carrying forth. One of the extraordinarily essential tools of meditation, of the dharma as it is written, is to interrogate. And what has gone awry in communities that have been developed and maintained by people who are holding white privilege is a refusal to interrogate certain areas.

There isn't an "Oh, only interrogate this." It's not taught to only interrogate emotions. You must interrogate your experience. Interrogate *all* of what you experience. Because yes, there's what's ultimate, and there's what's relative, so the only thing that should get left out of your interrogation are the things that you have no relationship to at all. Which basically is nothing.

I didn't leave anything out. I could have gone through those moments and decided, "I'm going leave the relationship I have to my partners out. I don't want to interrogate that. How convenient!"

As you interrogate, you recognize the places in which you're not interrogating, unless privilege allows you to avoid interrogation. That's the value of this kind of conversation, to remind us all that we don't have the right to do that, even as teachers. There's no teacher that can tell you, "Don't look at that." I think that's really important for people who feel like there's been a closing down of conversations in their communities— that you actually have to be responsible for your own liberation and your own practice and not turn over your liberation to the extent that you're being asked or required to not interrogate your reality.

RADICAL DHARMA: LOVE

Love can uproot fear or anger or guilt, because it is a greater
power. Love can go anywhere. Nothing can obstruct it.

—Sharon Salzberg

HEART TO HEART

REV. ANGEL: We open[ed] these conversations because we
realized that [it] is going to shift heart to heart. It's going to
shift at the deepest level.

We can have new legislation. We can put cameras on cops.
But it's going to be heart to heart that we expose these wounds.
We've all been wounded. We've all been wounded by structur-
al racism, but some of us got the more insidious version of it.

[Some of us] believe that we're smarter than people. We have
to control the room whenever we go in. We can't make mistakes. We can't get it wrong.

We have all been wounded by this.

If you're in this conversation, and you're not in this conversation with an intention towards love—with an intention
towards building and finding relationship—then it's not the
place for you to have the conversation. I hate saying that.

I want to have this fierce conversation with you because I
believe in connection as love, because I want to be liberated
from this space in which I have to disappear because you're
inhabiting that body like the pain, the guilt, the suffering, the
generations of pain and suffering, the generations of shame and
guilt. Like the [realization that] "Oh, my God. This has all been

going on and I'm grown up and haven't even seen this." That must just be devastating. I feel for white folks when I reach that place where I think, "Wow, I can't feel as you." But I feel for you. So we're suffering.

LAMA ROD: Mm-hm.

REV. ANGEL: And the only reason you should be in community spaces having the conversation is because you are invested in the community; you're invested in love. You're not just trying to teach somebody or fix someplace or something. If you're not coming to this from your open heart of love and desire to connect, even if it's funky and awkward and you can't get the words right and you mess it up, then you should go someplace else where you can actually feel safe enough and invested enough to have those conversations from a place of—a place of love towards love. From love towards love.

LAMA ROD: Mm-hm. Yeah, I think both of us get the label of being angry. That's why I have to keep saying "love." Traditionally for us, that's the way that people have shut us down. [They] put that wall up and go, "Oh, you're angry. You don't make any sense." That's why we've integrated love. But we have to practice through these labels of being angry.

REV. ANGEL: This is what's going to begin to shift hearts, when people have that moment of connection to their own human heart of, "Oh, I get that." That's why marriage equality was able to suddenly catch fire. It's not because a bunch of folks said, "Hey, I love me some gay people!"

People understood love. So there were unlikely allyships that were formed because many, many, many conservative, religious folks got to a place where what they heard was not "I now embrace gay people." They heard, "That's right. I don't want anyone infringing on my right to love." Because we all know love. And we all understand and have had some experience of the imposition on our hearts.

They were moved by the truth of the power of love and the "unwrangleability" of love. Because even when they might not have admitted it out loud, there are areas in which we can't wrangle our own love and it doesn't fit in a neat box. Whether people say that out loud or not, that's what they checked off at the ballot; that's where the legislation was able to move from.

So I encourage people to have conversations from the place of their own vulnerable hearts. I know that's scary, and I know that puts us on a line in a way, but I don't think that trying to have these conversations at the level of theory is going to work—intellectualizing is not going to be what moves people that are most resistant.

LAMA ROD: If you are a really well-positioned member of a *sangha*, make sure you're reaching out. If you're a person of color in a *sangha*, make sure you're reaching out to other new people of color coming through the door. Be the one who extends your hand and welcomes them and just talks openly. Model that kind of inclusivity for people.

WALK OUT

FEMALE SPEAKER: I am a member of the Baha'i community and also a member of the non-profit organization We Do Racial Healing Work. My husband and I are white, but our business partner is Black, and we work specifically on Black-and-white dynamics within the dharma community and also without. We have some similar issues in the Baha'i community.

Because we are so focused on the oneness of humanity, people think that, because I'm a Baha'i, I automatically don't have problems with racial prejudice—which is just not true. I'm very interested to see how other faith communities are dealing with this because we are trying to set an example in our community by being straightforward and talking about how white people engage in this, how Black people engage in this. I'm also just thrilled to meet other people that are doing this work in their faith communities.

LAMA ROD: What comes to mind is that taking care of ourselves is disruptive. The idea of self-care as a marginalized person or as a person of color or as a poor person—it's not the kind of nice self-care that you were talking about before but some sort of the fierce kindness of disrupting my routine, like I didn't go to work today. I needed to come here. Things like that, which there's a privilege in and is also a conscious sacrifice.

Self-care, I think, is a way of going against business as usual. It's a radical route. Learning to love ourselves is hard to do. It's a fierce kind of self-love that we need to work through—that I need to work through.

REV. ANGEL: I think that any form or any way in which you're not productive is disruption. Anything that takes you out of the system where you are producing something—I don't mean creating, I don't mean the things that nurture you and serve you and are generative for you—but when you drop out of the system and you are not productive, it will have consequences. But those consequences are part of the imagination of this system that says that we have to be producing and we have to be making something happen in order for us to have value, in order to effectively know who we are.

We also get kind of dramatic about self-care as something that needs to be partitioned off: I'm going to go to the spa! And the self-care can just be like, "Don't go." The ordinary day-to-day interruption and disruption is not happening enough. The protests are of value, but what's really overwhelming us is the ordinary day-to-day aggression that is not confronted right there on the spot. We are not risking ourselves for what we believe and for what we love.

LAMA ROD: Absolutely, and there's nothing wrong with the spa, as Jasmine and I know! We've been practicing radical self-care lately. But I think we're addicted to being triggered. It takes a choice to actually create these boundaries that produce suffering for us, and feel like we have to be hyper-vigilant to be in the world. We have to disrupt that.

I'm saying we need to take a break. We can't be on level ten all the time because that's running our bodies down, that's running our emotional/psychological state down. So you take those breaks and you put up those boundaries. You stay off Facebook, you don't answer the phone, you don't even text, you stay home if you can, you go for a walk, you go out to the woods, you do something. But we have been told in our radical communities that that is betrayal to the movement. So we're reproducing this blame, and we're actually reproducing shame. An activist radical community is sometimes the most brutal place to be in. How do we disrupt that in those spaces too?

REV. ANGEL: Yes, how do we disrupt this penchant we have for policing each other? Something that I see a lot is a sort of one-upmanship around having all the language right and being on all the fronts, because, if you have that all together, it really shows that you're radical. Of course, we want people to learn and to educate, but we also don't create any room so people that are trying to learn, and I want to say, especially white folks that are trying to learn, to understand how do I come to have a dialogue, to have a vocabulary about this? They can't get into the conversation because they don't already know what to say. That's kind of crazy. We're wagging our fingers because people don't already know, and then we're annoyed because they ask. Then we're upset because people didn't know, but we didn't want them to ask, and we're mad that they didn't already know. I mean, do you understand it's a circular conversation here?

That's true for folks of color too, because, frankly, we're all just swimming in the water. So folks of color don't just come with a vocabulary built in. It's an add-on purchase. And depending on where we're located and our economic situation and our skin color and our hair texture, we're getting different levels of confrontation with race. That isn't to say that any of us are escaping, because no one's escaping with race. I don't care how white you are or how Black you are; no one's escaping race in this society. It's a racialized society.

But we also have to demystify this notion that somehow people of color have all the information and know it all and white folks don't, and that it's just like Black and white.

Because it just isn't. We have to really allow ourselves to create some space for people not knowing, not understanding, just saying stupid things. I mean stupid as in ignorant. That's going to happen, and we have to figure out how to create room for that, rather than policing each other, so that people can actually get into the conversation.

If someone is asking, there's a willingness there. Treat that willingness as love, and treat it with love.

LAMA ROD: Because no one's born conscious. It's been a process for everyone. Personally, I've been a recipient of meanness. You have no idea what's going on, you don't know the language, you don't know the cause, but you want to learn, and that meanness, where you're told you're a part of the problem, that's like progressive radical elitism. We get too old for that sometimes. It's not productive. I need to be a part of spaces where I feel loved. And I don't feel loved in some of these spaces. Me leaving these spaces is self-care.

FEMALE SPEAKER: I think that in addition to self-care we need to take care of ourselves by taking care of each other. I say that as someone with a disability. It's a radical act to take care of each other, and it's a revolutionary act to ask others to take care of us. That's so much more powerful than self-care, and I think it's more in line with what we're cultivating here.

Also, as someone again who is disabled, I think there's often a conflation of discomfort with being unsafe. That's one of the things I often find myself communicating in multiracial spaces to white folks, that uncomfortable does not mean being unsafe. I once went to a normal day at Spirit Rock. It was appalling and frankly unsafe, but not in a physical way. I was not emotionally safe in that space, and I made the teacher uncomfortable. What do you do when you're the one making the teacher uncomfortable and they think that's unsafe or when you're making the dominant culture in the *sangha* uncomfortable and they're conflating it with safety and saying you're not actually promoting safety? How do you keep practice?

REV. ANGEL: Leave. Leave. What is your practice going to be made of if that's the condition?

We are a product of our conditions, and we're seeding our practice with the conditions in which we are growing our practice. So if you are putting down the seeds of your practice and having it grow in conditions that are so violent—it's not that it's just unsafe; it's violent. It's an assault on your being, and it's a restriction on the potential for your liberation, and so you must leave. You get out of spaces like that; it's a revolutionary act.

We have to stop martyring ourselves, and we actually have to disrupt spaces, and that means everyone, no matter what race you are. We have to disrupt spaces that are not seeking truth, that are not upholding our potential for liberation because they are invested in their comfort. Usually what that comfort means is that they are invested in perpetuating white supremacy. We have to disrupt them. And not disrupt them by trying to figure out how to be on their boards and trying to figure out how to do their diversity committees; we have to disrupt them by saying, "I am out." I'm not going to participate in this and letting them know why.

So it's not enough to walk out and protest in silence. Walk out and protest with some noise. Stand up in the room. This is particularly effective in dharma communities, where everyone is sitting silently and all you have to do is speak your truth in that room and say I cannot abide by this. I will not sit with this and so I will stand and leave. If we don't name it, it just keeps going.

One of the most powerful things that white folks can do is just call themselves white. Of course, it's not the whole of who you are, but neither is anyone's race the whole of who they are. But living and choosing to live in that discomfort of what gets foisted upon you right when you wear that label is stepping into a place of your own, as Lama Rod would say, being on your own frontlines and not trying to be on folks of colors' frontlines. Being on your own frontline is where the work is juiciest, and that's where it begins.

LAMA ROD: One of the kindest things that one of my teachers told me in my very first *sangha* was that you know you can leave, and it wasn't mean. We almost feel like there is nowhere else for us to go. There is. You have a practice, your own practice. It may be more difficult but you have your own experience to start working with. I really believe that if you have this authentic wish for practice, the community and the teachers will emerge eventually.

FEMALE SPEAKER: If one is caught in an abuse cycle, often one is paralyzed. So saying you just need to get up and leave— yeah, sure, but I'm still traumatized. And I'm sitting here and I'm feeling muted. How do you suggest that we develop the means to get up and leave?

LAMA ROD: Part of it has to do with trusting me. If I'm in that place and you're coming to me and I'm saying there's this pattern there, I think at some point you have to trust me enough. And start identifying more with this space of being loved, truly loved, and truly encouraged to be free and having the experience of what that means.

REV. ANGEL: One of the ways in which you can really hone your own power is to not have these conversations at all in places that you are not invested in and where there is not love. There are so many places that you have investment in—because it's your family, because it's your community where there is love—that you don't need to waste your energy having conversations with people and in situations in which there is not love.

One of the things that we really have to do that is completely radical is utterly invest ourselves in love and to continue to practice that. Then the tone of being in a place and in a situation in which there is not love and in which you are not held in love will be something you notice. That doesn't mean that you are always comfortable … with love also comes discomfort, but you'll be attuned enough to say, "Oh, when there's no love here, I don't even need to have this conversation."

What are you trying to prove to people where there is no love? Get out of that conversation. Just don't be there. Too many of us are doing that, and that's a result of our being habituated to suffering. We're habituated to being the victims of suffering, and we are habituated to being the perpetuators of suffering, so we go around and beat other people up that we have no investment in. I've watched so many people of color just banging their heads against that wall, trying to make those spaces change. That is deep, deep internalized oppression.

We are desperately trying to make our abusers love and accept us when they do not love and accept us without them doing their work, and you can't do their work for them. I don't care how much you want to love them into being. They have to do their own work, and so you have to really insist upon only living within the vibration of love. Love that changes, love that confronts, love that holds you, love that allows you to make mistakes but only within love.

LAMA ROD: But what if we've never been loved? Or what if we don't know what real love is? That's real for people. At least that was real for me in my practice early on. Because the way I was taught to love is by reproducing oppression and violence. I can't love you unless I'm getting something in return, or I'm going to cut you off unless you're doing something that I need. And that's the kind of love we're practicing consciously and unconsciously.

So how do you actually tune into authentic love, real love? The kind of love within Dr. King's speech? The love that isn't passive, but really direct and truthful and real? We suffer because we don't know how to do that, because we've been disenfranchised from love, which is part of why I think for marginalized people that's the way in which we still remain subjugated because we've been taught we have no right to love. Or be loved. For me interrogating that and starting to love myself is about developing an authentic understanding of love. When I knew what love was I knew people around me were actually trying to love me in a real way and I just couldn't get it before. Real teachers are trying to love you, but sometimes we sabotage that, and we go back to the people and the places that continually hurt us.

So how do we liberate ourselves from these cycles? It's really about believing in that real love and trusting it. Until you make that choice, you are bound in this cycle, and I can't pull you out physically because that becomes violence. I can't barricade the door of the *sangha* and keep you from going in, but I can continue to be a presence of authentic love. I look at it like it's a hamster cage. You have the wheel on the hamster cage and the hamster gets on and runs and even when the hamster jumps off, the wheel keeps spinning. I think that's what change is like: You may jump off that wheel that is reproducing this violence and it's going to keep spinning for a while, but it's going to slow down and stop eventually. We need to have the patience to wait. It takes time for love to sink in.

TRYING TO LOVE

FEMALE SPEAKER: I'm a disruptor. First, I just want to thank you, angel, Lama Rod, and everyone involved. I first want to express just the general impression upon me of the group of people that have gathered here tonight. Looking at us and our faces and our many shades, I think this is really beautiful and precious.

What's coming up for me is that we tend to use the language of separation when we're talking about skin privilege. There are different types of privilege across the board, so there's different types of oppression. Even if you are a straight, white male, this society is oppressing you in some way by dictating how and what you should be, and I acknowledge white supremacy is certainly alive and well in the Western world. There's also skin privilege in my home country of Argentina; there's skin privilege in my family system.

I'm brown, but I'm not the darkest person in my family. I'm mixed race. I'm Native American. I have a long line of Scots in my family. I've noticed it kind of feels good to be privileged. We go around the world; we go to other countries. I'm just going to call this out—we don't like to let go of our privilege, and when we feel more educated, more wealthy, more powerful, more privileged, there is a conscious awareness around not harming people, but we like our privilege.

Until we as brown people stop this type of dynamic, I feel like we're empowering the situation. We're sort of saying, "You have power over us. We have less value as people." So, when do we claim our power or when do we decide we have value? People will continue to see us as less valuable if we continue to say, "You are the privileged and powerful." When do we decide we are people of all colors with varied experiences going in all directions? How do we acknowledge what's happening?

REV. ANGEL: For me, naming the social reality of the privilege of white skin is not giving it power. I'm naming a social reality. I think it's important to do that because too many of us are not aware of it and don't acknowledge the impact that it has on people. That's very distinct from saying that it defines who I am. But I have to navigate against that because I operate in society, after all.

I think my depth of practice and my own just enormous

personal power lets me get by a lot of things. So I have the experience of that particular paradox. When you are steeped and rooted in your own power, a lot of the perceived dynamics of what's coming at you actually changes because you don't let it. I don't make space for a whole bunch of bullshit, and so it doesn't come for me. There's no room here for this, but I can still catch a bullet if I open my mouth in the way I tend to open my mouth to a white cop. That's not giving them power. That cat has a gun and he's been socialized to view my Black female queer body as beneath him. As a result, he devalues the life that exists in this body, and therefore is willing to take that life wantonly.

One of the challenges we have is that to name it *is* to give it power. I think the way that we name it invites those people that are swimming in it, without knowing they are swimming in it, because many people that are within white-skinned privilege are upholding privilege even though they don't have white skin. The real problem is that they're not recognizing the suffering that they're experiencing as a result. They're not recognizing how they're cut off from love and loving and how that cut-offness from love is not limited to how they are relating to dark brown and Black-skinned people.

It's actually representing itself in their family lives, and that's why there's such a high degree, I believe, of mental illness that runs through white America, such a high level of psychopathic behavior, because there's so much repressed.

I was saying this at a gathering I was at the other day. I don't think we're better people in this era if, as human beings, we have the same hearts fundamentally as human beings that existed in other times. What happened to people? What did they have to do to be born, live, and die watching Black bodies sold on the corner like popcorn or cotton candy or a cell phone cover? What kind of cut-offness had to happen for generations in order for people to abide by that?

These are bodies. It's not like you can kind of *pretend* that they're *not* bodies. They have arms and legs. All the parts look the same. They're just darker; their hair is kinkier, but they are human bodies. White folks need to inquire into what is running through their generational line as a result of whiteness, what had to happen for people to see that and to live with that for generations. Not just focus on what has happened to us, but what has happened to *you*. So I'm not talking about giving people power. I'm actually encouraging people to take back their own power by taking back the wholeness of who they are by examining and interrogating what this system has done, not to just whoever is marginalized but to the people that are participating and perpetuating that marginalization … often unbeknownst to them.

FEMALE SPEAKER: I totally hear what you're saying, and I'm sorry. With all due respect, I'm all for one people and all of that, but we need to get down to really have the conversations that are necessary because the inclination to bypass is so strong. Not to bypass, but to acknowledge. For instance, there's Jewish folks who are lighter skinned. There's Armenian folks who are lighter skinned, who've all gone through persecution and genocide, and so what I'm saying is that there's sort of a universal experience. We're kind of narrowing our conversation to what's happening. I think it's really necessary to think about how to stop thinking that we're separate, that there are different people.

JASMINE: One of the things you're walking into is a weekend-long retreat dedicated to radical dharma race, love, and liberation. One of the things that happens in both dharma communities and academic communities is this attempt to view the problem of suffering and of racial violence in a "we all experience it" kind of way. I think that's true, and systems impact different people differently. I'm impacted differently because of my gender and my race and my class and education. All of those factors matter, so when we talk about Black Lives Matter, it's the materiality of our embodiment that actually matters, on the level of domination and empowerment. Those are the things that we have to attend to. I don't know that we have the tools necessary to acknowledge that in our own families.

My sister is impacted by race more than I am. Our families are constructed in ways that completely black out the ways in which violence impacts us differently. Part of what I'm interested in talking about is how we can love each other through that imbalance. I don't know how to make up for it. I don't know how to change it, but I do know I can stare at my sister and say, "I see that you are impacted differently than me, and I'm going to stand with you in whatever way you need me to stand with you and create communities in spaces that would honestly rather us be completely alienated and alone and isolated from each other."

I'm all for the end game, the utopia, but I also know that the way we are going to get there requires that we deal with the fact that we are very different and have different experiences. In my classes, I ask the students to tell each other our stories, and then we talk about the ways in which our personal stories are politicized and constructed by different systems of power in different ways, that those stories are interconnected. I'm trying to see the ways we can build connection without obliterating difference.

FEMALE SPEAKER: In that video of your interview [the original *Buddhadharma* interview with Lama Rod and Rev. angel described at the beginning of this section], I think you were talking after Michael Brown was shot and expressing your feelings. You had white congregational members come up and say, "But we love you." You said, "That's not sufficient." That just grabbed me, and I wanted to hear you speak to that. When we do this work, we find it's really the white men who don't show up.

LAMA ROD: I attract a lot of white men. It's really interesting.

REV. ANGEL: So do I … I'll have to trade notes with you. [Laughter]

LAMA ROD: Middle-aged white men really seek me out for teaching. Not queer-identified either—straight, middle-class white men. There's a study there that I have to do at some point. [Laughter] Getting back to that question: angel was present, we were actually together the day we found out about Robin Williams, which affected how I was operating. [There was] also everything happening in Ferguson, the military attacks in Palestine. With Robin Williams actually reintroducing depression and mental illness, I was triggered really strongly and a lot of trauma stuff was coming up for me.

When I would share that, I felt like people would shut down. As a response people would simply say, "Oh, but I love you," as if what I was experiencing was wrong or unrelatable to them. I think what I was looking for was simply the space to be held. Not to be told, "You'll be OK." I just wanted to experience what I was experiencing in community. I know people love me, but we get into these situations where we feel like we have to say something, instead of being vulnerable and allowing ourselves not to know what to do. Plenty of times people come up to me and I have no idea what to say. I just sit with them. It's all I can do.

So it can be hurtful. Especially if you're not really deeply embodied in that expression of love—when you're using that expression simply to mask discomfort, to deflect. That was the hurtful part for me. These were friends, *sangha* members, who were saying that, and that's why I was so uncomfortable. I know they love me, but I knew that's not what I needed. You didn't have to say that.

SPEAKER: Thank you.

REV. ANGEL: Thank you all so much.

RADICAL DHARMA: LIBERATION

*One of the extraordinary things about liberation is that you
do not feel the need to control things when you're free, because
the illusory nature of control becomes clear to you.*

—REV. ANGEL KYODO WILLIAMS, SENSEI

WHAT DOES LIBERATION LOOK LIKE, AND WHERE DOES IT LIVE?

*Black women are the canary in the coal-mine of the social
structure of America, and as the canaries, they seek the air that
is most clear, because they know what it's like to suffocate.
They know what it's like to suffocate as women, people in
female-gendered bodies; they know what it's like to suffocate
as people in Black-skinned bodies, and so, as people that have
touched the liberatory teachings—when they seek liberation,
when they seek a clear space to breathe—they create that space
around everyone because they know what it's like to suffer, to
suffocate.*

*In the teachings of the Dharma, the first teaching is that life is
suffering. It's not a thought, it's not an idea, it's not something
that you should take as you go off onto the second Noble
Truth—it's teaching. It's something that you actually have to
come to know. And if you don't truly know, know intimately
that "life is suffering," then you cannot know what it means
to seek liberation. So Black female bodies know suffering; that
is the nature of their existence in this society—they know*

suffering. Therefore, they know liberation when they see it and they are not capable of not seeking that liberation on behalf of others. Because that's what liberation is; that's what liberation actually gives rise to. You can't possibly come to know the depths of suffering and then have any wish other than to not only be free of your own suffering, but to have others be free of their suffering. Because of who they are in society, they have to do that.

—Rev. angel Kyodo williams, Sensei
from an interview with Professor Felicia Sy

"THE PEOPLE OF COLOR PROBLEM"

REV. ANGEL: What I get to hear is largely about white folks who are trying to figure out how to fix the people of color problem. That's what people ask me all the time: How do we invite more people of color? What I don't hear in that is: "I'm suffering. I'm experiencing trauma. What is it that I can do to help myself?"

LAMA ROD: I think it says a lot about *sanghas* when the line is, "Well, we need to be more diverse. How do we get brown bodies into these seats?" I don't care about brown people populating the *sangha* because that's a distraction for me. I am interested in the healing piece. I'm interested in looking at how we're suffering, how we're creating these relationships that actually exclude people. I don't use the word "diversity." I really rarely use the word "racism." I think we have this programmed response to these words, and we have to disrupt that by transforming the language a little bit or by using more precise language. The suffering of whiteness. The trauma of whiteness. Let's look at our suffering. How do we practice in such a way that we're restoring our humanity? How can we instigate that kind of transformation? Because healing is also transformation.

REV. ANGEL: How do we practice in such a way that we restore humanity? That suggests that our humanity has been compromised. That the humanity of white folks, in particular, has been compromised.

LAMA ROD: Well, the humanity of this country *is* compromised. One of the sisters over here spoke about embracing our history—which is an act of reconciliation. How do we say that our country is really a very violent place? We have a very violent history. We can wave the flag around and talk about democracy. How can we use the reconciliation models that we've been seeing in other countries, like South Africa, for instance? That's healing, you know? That's saying, "Oh, there's trauma."

We have historical trauma as a country, as communities, as different-bodied people, as different racially identified people. There's trauma we have to start bringing to the surface and articulating the hurt, the guilt, the pain—holding the space for that. I don't see that happening in communities.

REV. ANGEL: For too long these conversations have circulated around the healing that has to be done for people of color. Even reconciliation. Even South Africa. The lens that is conventionally held is that there's healing to be done, but largely that healing is to be done on *behalf* of people of color. I may have to say I'm sorry as a white person. I may have to deal with some guilt and shame. But who's really being impacted has heavily focused on people of color, "different" people. "Oh, women are suffering. Oh, queer people are suffering. Oh, Black people are suffering."

But for me, too, there's been too little conversation allowing space for the unearthed suffering of white folks. Almost because of the power dynamics involved and almost because we have been so racialized into saying, "If I'm white, I'm supposed to feel bad for folks of color." But there's zero space for white folks to really claim suffering around living in a racialized society. There's no space, it seems to me, for white people to actually get down to the conversation. Even folks sitting there are feeling it and they're, like, "Hm, I better not say anything." It can't even be acknowledged that there is any suffering. I just don't see how we can ever expect that this dynamic is going to change if we can't allow people to fully claim their own suffering.

That's what the dharma is actually about. It's about allowing people the space and the opportunity for discomfort so that they can touch their own suffering. And this focus on other people's suffering, for me, frankly, feels like a distraction. It feels like we have spent decades now tiptoeing around other people's discomfort. I think there's some degree of relief that people feel. I think some relationships may grow in those conditions. But in my own experience, when the shit hits the fan and people are in contraction, when the economy turns upside down, when the spaces that people live in start to change, when more people of color—more marginalized people—enter the room, when people contract, they go back to those places of unaddressed suffering and the behaviors that we experience as racialized behavior, like micro-aggressions, and so on, continue.

So we can all be on good behavior, and I feel that that's what we've had in the dharma for the last forty years. Good behavior dharma. It's largely progressive—not 100 percent—and we have this progressive liberal way of talking about race, either

I'm color-blind or "I'm OK with colored folks" in theory. But the reality is that people of color are not feeling welcome. They're not feeling welcome, and they're not feeling welcome because there aren't enough POC scholarships! [Laughter]

DEFINING LIBERATION

LAMA ROD: I'm listening to where people are coming from, and I notice a lot of frustration, anger, and helplessness. This is actually a deepening orientation towards healing.

In our conversation we're defining and identifying it as "liberation." You can ask, "What is liberation? What are we liberating ourselves from?" We're actually going through frustration, anger, helplessness to be liberated. We're developing the capacity to experience all of this in a direct way. Often when we run into the difficult stuff, we actually just set it to the side and then somehow define that as healing.

This is a lot of what we find with the practice of color-blindness. We're just going to put it to the side where we don't see it: "There's no color! There's no system there! There's nothing. We just don't see it anymore." We have to really challenge that because we're not opening to difference and how we're affected by difference. How we're benefiting from difference. How we're not benefiting from difference.

In Theravadan Buddhism there are two kinds of *sukha*, or happiness: our outer happiness and our inner happiness. Outer happiness is related to the external world, to our stuff, to situations, to things that give us joy, like Netflix and Hulu. This is Brooklyn, I guess, so maybe composting and dogs and babies.
REV. ANGEL: Walking dogs.
LAMA ROD: Local handcrafted beers and stuff. That gives

us joy. That outer stuff. Our cars. Our houses. Our status. And that's where we're stuck. That's just superficial happiness. We're cycling through that. I call that *samsara*. That's ignorance until we begin to see what it really is. Then we can start moving into that inner happiness, which is the recognition of the natural state of being, the natural state of mind.

We have to see this first-level happiness isn't ultimate happiness. That comes with a lot of discomfort. I go back to this analogy of the lotus in the mud. The lotus actually emerges from the mud. So we're talking about wisdom emerging from the chaos, the ignorance, the suffering because we're learning to transform this relationship to what is around us. We're not so clingy and attached to the outer part of this first level of happiness. We begin to interrogate that. In doing so, we're allowing space for discomfort to be there, and we're developing real awareness of what happiness is. But we have to see through that discomfort. As we begin to see through it, we begin to transform that relationship.

"A KINDER, GENTLER SUFFERING"

LAMA ROD: The question I have is when is enough enough? When do we finally start making the choices to confront, to interrogate, and to strategize around the forces of hate and materialism and devaluing? How do we create antidotes to the otherness that many of us feel in our communities? How do we practice self-agency and reimagining our lives, not within the context of someone else's imagination but within our own? Not within an imagination that is about control and domination, about silence and hate, especially self-hate. How do you take that power away from people?

These are the questions I started with when I began my dharma practice those dozen or so years ago. I wanted to seek refuge; I wanted peace from the overwhelming trauma of being all these identities. I was seeking liberation from this deep, deep hunger, this deep, deep sense of loneliness, this deep, deep sense of feeling like I didn't matter, that I wasn't important, that no one cared. What I was able to see was that liberation was up to me, and that's what my early dharma teachings were really about. Liberation was a choice, and at some point I had to choose liberation on my own.

REV. ANGEL: I want to chime [in] because what I hear a lot is people asking questions about navigating their dharma centers and their spiritual homes, and about what *those* people are doing rather than [people] taking responsibility for themselves.

What we're missing in dharma communities is that people seem to have forgotten that this is about liberation. And that is a significant challenge I see all over the place. I think that we're settling for this as a result of white-skin privilege and white supremacy and the complacency it engenders. We've ended up settling for a kinder, gentler suffering rather than actually seeking and seeing our practice in our communities and our *sanghas* as places for liberation.

It's—as this young brother said when I was at Buddhafest [a conference held in DC]—like a white finishing school, and people are just figuring out how to be nicer to each other. But it's all within those confines of Puritan values of whiteness foisted upon the country at large, which are to not interrupt, to not confront, to not challenge, to not say things when you see things. Because I guarantee you that most of the racism that is occurring, and most of the really pervasive presence of white supremacy that gives rise to the discomfort that we're feeling and the misalignment that we're feeling in our communities, is happening in the presence of perfectly good people who know better, that know this is not what they want to see in themselves. But we've all acquiesced to minding our business. And that's not liberation.

LAMA ROD: Part of me wants to articulate this experience of feeling colonized within American Buddhism. Rev. angel and myself, we have to have a practice to sit here and talk about white supremacy and racism and valuing others, but even if we do this in a loving way, there are still people who will resist it and still call it aggressive. When we start talking about how these kinds of systems and structures are reproduced in *sanghas*, then we are met with this wall: "Why are you being aggressive, why are you being angry, why are you yelling?" Meanwhile, you haven't even raised your voice yet.

"THE REAL THING"

FEMALE SPEAKER: Thank you so much for having this conversation today. The discomfort—I really identify with that. And I think feeling discomfort and being in it is healing. I truly believe that with all my heart.

I think the biggest disease in America—because this is where I live; I haven't really lived anywhere else—is consumption. It's such a distraction. I identify with some of what other people said, not being able to process feelings. There's young men who come from families where men are still being told not to be in touch with their feelings. Being in discomfort is very healing.

FEMALE SPEAKER: With regard to how diversity's taken in the dharma, what I find is that there is not a recognition or an understanding that one's background and one's nationality, one's whiteness forms a lens through which we read the teachings. The communities may want to include people of color and more diversity; what I come up against is them not realizing what that's going to do in terms of exposing how they're actually holding the dharma. Once you bring in more diverse cultures—peoples that are holding wisdom from other spiritual traditions, from their other own lineages, from their own cultures—their wisdom is coming from their experiences of being Black, as being Asian, as being queer.

Whatever the aspects are that are the most uncomfortable are the aspects that probably should be that person's practice. But, like you said, there's this generation of teachers of color and students that are starting to leave because the way oppression exists is making people not feel safe enough to go through the teacher trainings, and they're bouncing.

FEMALE SPEAKER: Thanks for being here. Wonderful to have this event. I'm a believer and I've been a participator in white ally groups and *sanghas* and allied and POC groups. I've been impressed with the importance of relationship and connecting through dialogue. I wonder, aside from doing specific identity work, what can we do about coming together during what can often be a quiet non-relational time together? Do we need more spaces to talk within *sanghas* and not just be quiet and listen to one person? I'm just curious about where the potential is for relationships to be built?

LAMA ROD: I absolutely believe that we can use the quiet or the sitting practice to avoid having the dialogue. I am trying to resist going into quiet sitting practice to avoid feeling uncomfortable. I've tried to have more dialogue in my *sanghas*, or anywhere I teach, actually, because I think that's what we're really craving. People can sit at home in quiet, but in community we need to know where we are and how we are. And I think that when we really engage dialogue around difference, we can really deepen our relationships. I think there's particular work that different people need to do in that engagement of difference.

REV. ANGEL: Meditation is not the primary practice for most Buddhists in the world. The thick number of people who practice meditation would be here in the States and in the UK. I think it's not an accident that white convert *sanghas* are putting such a strong emphasis on non-relational ways of developing their *sanghas*. I'm not saying there's anything wrong with meditation, but I think that's our mistake.

We can use anything, even a practice of liberation, to further our neuroses. What walking the Buddha's path calls us to do is to shine the light on the path of neuroses and to do exactly the opposite. We don't have to know what the outcome is; we just have to know we have a neurosis around hyper-individualism in this society and disconnection and distraction and that we are increasingly out of relationship with each other, no matter how many Facebook friends we have.

It's also not an accident that by contrast Black and brown folks mostly hail from oral traditions, and so there is a discomfort that arises just out of that cultural difference. It has occurred to me that one of the challenges of white privilege is how few white folks realize that other folks have different cultural practices and ways of being—that their way isn't The Way and that everyone else is somehow different and off … which suggests that difference is "off" from the real thing.

I was going to say earlier on that white folks got the privilege of bringing the dharma into America, and they got to shape it, got to interpret it, and got to choose which aspects of the text would be highlighted, which aspects of the teachings, and which orientation of spaces would be brought to the forefront. Ultimately, I don't think people are doing that because they need to oppress. I think they do it because they are engaged in their neurosis, to repress feeling their own experiences of disconnection, their own sense of being lonely. Rather than using the practice to go into it and connect, we're furthering that neurosis.

We can't save everyone that's going to bounce because of what they're experiencing. Dedicated practitioners, the dharma's in your heart. The truth is in your heart. The love of that is in your heart. It's going to be a small group of us. Some of us come with the resilience, and that will help make room for some people that have a little less resilience. Some people will build the resilience, and we will increasingly make room for people that have different expressions and interpretations. It's going to be a process. We have to, as Rod was saying, form community to create supportive and expressive and creative spaces for people that are marginalized in all sorts of ways. We will crack the ceiling.

MALE SPEAKER: I was just thinking about the [dharma] tradition over the past one hundred years and the reaction that African Americans or Blacks and the diaspora have had to being closed out or feeling uncomfortable in institutions. I think there's one where you fight for a space within institutions, but also there's another where we form our own. I would love to hear your thoughts of what that would look like. I don't know if a lot of whites in this room know, but when we're together, there's so many African and traditional spiritual Caribbean practices and experiences that we bring to the Buddhist practice. I'm curious in the next twenty, thirty years how the practice is going to look and feel with all of our traditions included into it.

LAMA ROD: The practice I bring from the diaspora is always being late to everything. [Laughter] I'm five minutes late to my *sangha*. And there's a search party going down. But this is how I was raised.

I do a lot to bring traditions from the diaspora into the way that I teach, into the way that I am within *sanghas*. And there's resistance to that, but I feel like there's beginning to be more reception because there's a lot of healing in what we're bringing from our tradition. I think in the future we will see communities that are much more embracing.

I grew up in the Black church, and I still have that in my heart. I love a little fellowship dinner after *sangha*. "Fellowship" is a really important word for me. We're in community. We're relating to one another. We're trying to support each other in healing and in having this space to support one another in life transitions. I want to bring pieces of the congregational model into traditional *sanghas*.

REV. ANGEL: I think what that looks like is going to change as more of us become teachers. This engages the power position question. By nature of the limited number of loosely sanctioned teachers of color, there's a limit to peer-led *sanghas*. Communities get to natural limits, so in terms of the people that want to go deeper in the practice, not fellowship, people can be peer-led forever. As they want to deepen their practice, they're going to run into the ceiling of wanting and needing guidance that comes from having studied teachers. So for now, there's going to be a little bit of a ceiling because we have to wait for a new rising of teachers of color. And then I think there's going to be an interesting churn. Because one of the challenges that comes through the fact of white folks having carried many of these traditions over is an obsession with authenticity.

That obsession with authenticity has very much more to do with trying to locate oneself when whiteness is all we've been left with, because this country needed to cut people off from heritage and needed to cut people off from lineage in order to organize them, explicitly against brown, Black, and red peoples. So the obsession with authenticity says that's not real this and that's not real that. Any one of us that does any study of the history of Buddhism knows that what it is best at is picking up other traditions as it goes along. As we simultaneously slough off the cultural baggage of whatever mother countries these practices have come from, we're going to have to start letting other things in, including, in this country, the teachings which happen all over Africa. As it is, I've seen it in South Africa— Buddhist *sanghas* with predominantly Black-bodied people in them. They have diasporic practices. It raises questions about what the invisibility of whiteness has robbed from white people that would have allowed them to more naturally express their own manifestation of the dharma.

LAMA ROD: Going back to this practice of Black prophetic tradition, I think teachers of color, especially Black teachers, really have to return to that kind of way of being in spiritual community which isn't aggression, but is something about how we're embodying and speaking to that embodiment. That's important. I don't see a lot of teachers of color in general, but I think from the few Black teachers I've seen, I feel we could be doing more to embody that Black prophetic fire.

We've lost that radicalism, and we've kind of succumbed a little bit to some of these really harsh realities of being marginalized in *sanghas*, though we have some teaching authority. My question is always, how do we regain that prophetic vision, that fire, to use the words of Professor Cornel West, that prophetic,

Black tradition? How do we return it to that in a way that's not materialistic or self-serving?

I think the directors of centers can do what they will, but teachers have a responsibility to speak truth in the best way that they can in the service of people's happiness, to giving people an opportunity to see and experience what they need to see and experience in order to transcend their suffering. First, to be honest about their suffering, then to actually develop a relationship to that suffering, and then to work with the suffering and work through the suffering. You can't actually go to the other end automatically. Too often we're selling the idea that we can just skip over the suffering part. And if you put your money in the *dana* basket or fill out your membership form and pay your dues, it's all taken care of, and we can sit here and we can be nice with each other. We avoid causing one another any discomfort because if we did, we'd remind ourselves of the suffering that we're actually experiencing.

If we're asked to check our suffering at the door, then what are we here for? And I think that this is probably, for me, one of the strongest inhibitions to being able to get to truth, to get to the Radical Dharma. Folks are worried about their own sixty-five-million-dollar jets. If I'm more worried about having people and their money over being as honest as I can, then we're in trouble.

We're not talking about just roughing people up for the sake of it, but that's what we're doing. We're bean-counting. And part of that comes out of the fact of Buddhism's arriving in a cultural context in which there is not an automatic understanding in the larger cultural context about the relationship between the teachers and the community. Historically, teachers have been supported by the community, and so lacking that, we have unfortunately deferred to a capitalization of our teaching. We've commercialized and moved our dharma teaching into a capitalist model of competition, marketing, who sells the best, and then ego just runs rampant.

Our integrity is compromised when we're dependent upon our communities for support. Now obviously relationship is important. At the same time, we have to be careful about how we compromise our vision for liberation. When we compromise, we're actually compromising liberation for both ourselves and for the people we're in service to. That's something I've had to really reflect on. Do I say what I need to say? Or do I censor what I feel like I need to say in order to keep people coming to see me?

I think I've been very fortunate on my path not to be so supported by *sangha*. So I've never had that thing where I was like, "Oh, I'm getting all the support. I better not say anything." I wasn't getting supported fully, so I just felt like I could say what I wanted to. But over time, what I began to witness is that people were actually hungry for that kind of authenticity. That's exactly why I entered into relationship with my own teachers. Because finally there were people in my own life who loved me enough to tell me the truth, who didn't beat around the bush. My root teacher does not beat around the bush. He just points it out: This is where you need the work. He doesn't care about people not supporting him; he cares about you being liberated. I think any authentic spiritual teacher is concerned with your liberation.

REV. ANGEL: Period.

LAMA ROD: I feel like that's why we're willing to do it. You should do this only because you want to see people liberated and happy. I think this is important because being liberated means to be happy, and to be happy means we are liberated or at least in process.

REV. ANGEL: Not "happy" in the ordinary sense. I think even when we say "happiness is important," it's important for people to know what we mean by "happiness" because it's not an ordinary happiness.

LAMA ROD: The happiness that I'm talking about is that deep sense of well-being, comfort—not materialistic comfort but that deep sense of being at home with who and what you are. Occupying that space in a way that's not dependent on the external environment, that's not dependent on your Honda or your 65-million-dollar jet or where you live. It's dependent on being fundamentally OK with who you are—no matter if you are experiencing tragedy, illness, death—you're always at home with that. And when I'm at home, there's a sense of spaciousness. So I can be happy at the same time I can be going through rage and anger and despair.

I'm not saying you can't have a secondary level of happiness that we get from our Hondas and our jets and our favorite TV shows and our ice cream. The joy we get from our puppies and cats when we go home. Because sometimes those are the only friends we have; those are the only creatures that will put up with us. But really they're just dependent on us, so they know enough to act right because they need to get fed. So we have this secondary happiness that comes from relationships, that comes from other things but that can't be primary because that doesn't last. Whatever's created will be destroyed, so nothing will last. That's why we ground ourselves in a sense of being at home in our own experience, in who and what we are. That's the happiness I'm talking about. Relationships with spiritual teachers and so forth helps us to develop a relationship to that inner happiness.

"WHAT ARE YOU WILLING TO GIVE UP?"

LAMA ROD: We're not here to reproduce comfort. You can go to a country club for that. Or you can go to the club; you can go out to the bar, which we all do. Sometimes our *sanghas* are country clubs. This is not a social club. This is not a country club. I mean, there's snacks and drinks and everything; that's fine. But this is a place for us to be uncomfortable, and for it to be safe to be uncomfortable, because discomfort is where liberation really emerges from, just like the Buddhist symbol of the lotus that emerges from the mud. We need to emerge from our confusion through strategies of awareness. You can't emerge from something you haven't owned and recognized. What we are seeing now, instead of folks owning that confusion, is that we try to bypass the chaos of the mud or the confusion because we see *sanghas* as being this really nice place we can relax, but it doesn't serve us actually. Like I said, you can relax anywhere. We waste *sangha* and community when we choose not to engage in discomfort associated with liberatory practice.

REV. ANGEL: The misunderstanding is that refuge means somehow being protected from our discomfort. Refuge is actually about being protected from all of the things that are hindering our ability to see our discomfort and to be able to actually come in contact with it. The refuge is: Here is a space. Here is an opportunity for you to meet your discomfort instead of continuing to bypass it, to drug it, to distract from it, to Hulu it or to Facebook it or—you know all of the ways.

We're always talking about other forms of anesthetizing ourselves. We create this separation between people who are drug users and alcoholics, so they're the bad ones that aren't taking care of themselves and are really distracted. In fact, we are all heavily anesthetized by the various ways we're distracted from our own suffering. Mine is maybe online shopping, but we all have some version of it and just because we're not actually using hard drugs or hard alcohol doesn't mean that we're not distracting ourselves from this pain.

Not the least of which is to recognize our distraction from how deeply misaligned most of our communities are—that we're waving the flag of wisdom and compassion, and we can't stop pulling ourselves in when someone "other" comes in, whether that "other" is a brown or Black body or a transgender body. That's a significant challenge because we don't confront it. It's a challenge because folks are so desperate to fit in and to find a place of relative ease that we begin to acquiesce our own power and what we know is right, and our own wisdom and our own truth just so that we can belong. And it's really, really time for us to break with that and question, what are you belonging to?

LAMA ROD: What are you belonging to and also what are you willing to give up? I think that disruption comes at a price, and for many of us to really call out injustice means that we risk belonging in certain communities, belonging within our families, belonging within our friend groups, belonging within our *sanghas*, belonging within our workplaces. You know wherever a community is for you, and that's a really hard choice.

REV. ANGEL: We're way too invested in nation-building around Buddhism and nation-building around these institutions, in general. We're more invested in some sense of continuity because we have a fear of death. Because we're invested in extending continuity beyond this current moment, we can't just have our dharma practice in our living rooms and forget about high rents, and forget landlords and all of the things that we have to pay for. We need to figure out how we just create real true *sangha* wherever it is that we are.

LAMA ROD: The struggle with that is that we're not seeing examples of this. Because some of us don't even know how to do that. How do we actually project a sense of authenticity into the world? We have no idea who we are because no one's showing us. We're distracted by these things because we prioritize and value trying to fit in, trying to belong, instead of actually privileging our deepest desires for equality, equanimity, community. And I think that for those of us who struggle there's a lot to learn from others who have made these choices before, to privilege who and what they are at whatever cost that comes.

REV. ANGEL: Do you have some examples?

LAMA ROD: Anyone who we see as a hero. I think we are drawn to their choice that they made to be themselves. There are all kinds of examples. Personally, of course, my teachers, and before even coming in the dharma, just the great change-makers like, for instance, Ericka Huggins, who some of you know. I just met her today but have known her through correspondence for a while. She is someone who I've followed for a while and just sitting with her today and asking her what was that choice for her? When did she choose to privilege her deepest desires to create change?

If you know her, and know of her story, as one of the leaders of the Black Panthers in the '60s right here in your community, it cost her a lot. Regardless of what she lost, she was always coming back to help people. And ultimately, I think for me that's truly the bottom line. What am I doing to benefit myself and others?

There's a sense of integrity too, as Rev. angel was pointing out. I think the choice that I had to make was that I had to value and choose integrity. Doing what I needed to do to support the benefit of my students and those around me over whatever financial benefit there was. And I think that when we choose other things over integrity, that's when the violence starts in our communities and our relationships. I don't want to say that it's so widespread, but I think that's the root of so much violence in our relationships with our spiritual teachers. When that integrity gets devalued and you become a source of something that the teacher needs. I don't need anything from you. I need you to practice. If you want to give me a few dollars fine, but I'm not in it for that.

REV. ANGEL: Too many of us as dharma teachers have also given up our authenticity because our livelihood is tied to people's feeling of being comfortable. Too many of us are more and more willing to allow a kinder, gentler suffering. Just give people a little bit of a salve, a little bit of a balm on their suffering, and not really touch the place of challenge and woundedness that needs to be touched to release the energy so that people can actually find their liberation.

So if you're going to dharma communities, if you're going to walk in the path of the Buddha, if you're going to any place of spiritual enrichment in which you are not meaningfully experiencing discomfort, not all the time, but meaningfully uncomfortable frequently, you are not doing your work, and you are not walking the path of liberation. I just want to let you know that. If it's all warm and fuzzy all the time, then someone is really not dropping wisdom. Otherwise, it just means that we're all sitting in here awake already. Right? Because that's about the only time that it should stay warm and fuzzy, is if we're already awake.

If that's not what's happening, if you're not being challenged, if you're not feeling uncomfortable, and particularly made uncomfortable by the teacher, someone's dropping the ball. I'm not saying you're wasting your time. Maybe you want kinder, gentler suffering. Maybe that's what you're in it for. But if it's liberation you're after, and you're not experiencing discomfort, liberation is not where you're headed. You just need to know that.

LAMA ROD: Even two days ago [before the Charleston massacre,] you all needed a space to grieve; we always need spaces to grieve because we don't have public spaces to grieve anymore. We do not like to do public mourning in our country, in our world. We are really uncomfortable around grieving people and sickness and death, so we send it off somewhere. That's trauma. We're told, "Oh, you can't be sad. You can't be upset. You can't be sensitive to the suffering of the world because that makes people uncomfortable. You're not going to be productive if you're sitting around weeping all the time."

Rev. angel and I can hold the space for this pain because we hold the space for our own suffering, because that's been the stuff, the material, of our practice.

REV. ANGEL: Many of us don't feel permission.

You have to disrupt business as usual in your own life, and you have to disrupt business as usual in all of the spaces that you're in. If you don't do anything tonight, leave here anointed as a disruptor, and really allow the rest of our time together to embolden you, to strengthen that resolve in you to disrupt on the spot and to make people uncomfortable. Give yourself permission to be uncomfortable and to make others uncomfortable in your truth.

LAMA ROD: I'm an activist, so I can say this: sometimes we go to do the easy stuff. Let's go to a march, let's go plan something, but meanwhile we can't even talk to our friends and families. We can't even be ourselves and have that courage in our meetings to stand up and say, "I don't agree with this. Let's do something different. I believe in love, not this aggression." That's the kind of disruption we're talking about. You can do everything else, but let's start with the basics.

To be a bodhisattva in the world—which doesn't mean necessarily that I have to be like Jesus, that I have to sacrifice myself—we have to ask, "How do I witness the violence in the world? How do I do what I can do to disrupt that violence, and how do I work in a very skillful way in whatever way possible? How do we hold space for our own rage and despair?"

In my practice I ask, "Why am I always so interested in fixing and channeling my rage into something else?" Why am I always so fixated on this? Why am I giving it all this narrative and airtime? Why am I making it the heart of my presence in the world? Why can't it just be this experience? Why does it always have to be there in everything and all of my interactions? Where does love come in? Can't love and rage exist together? How do I take care of my rage? These are just questions that I go through in my own practice, but at the end of the day, whatever it is, I just have to know, I just have to be there. There will always be violence because there will always be a *samsara*. There will always be ignorance.

For many of us who are on the streets, on the frontlines— we're getting burned out. We are getting run-down. We are being killed. We are being confiscated by states and empire. And when I'm at actions and protests, people are like, "Oh, what are you doing here? Shouldn't you be in the *zendo*?" I say, "No, I study Buddhism in *zendos*, but my practice compels me to be in the world because I don't have a choice. I'm Black too. It doesn't matter if I'm walking outside with this shawl on. I'm still a Black man with a shawl on. My body could still take a blow just like any other person if people assume things about me that aren't true, so I have to be real about that.

I see too many people who will not think twice about going out to the march, and to the die-in and to all these great fun things we do as activists, but aren't willing to talk about these issues with the people that live with them. And I think our activism has to be about equipping ourselves with the tools to have the conversations with the people that are closest to us, because these people will listen to us much more than they would someone else that's further from them.

In the classroom, one strategy that has really been helpful for me is to actually articulate my experience with my professors. I had a particular incident on the day that the grand jury decided not to indict the officer [who shot Michael Brown], and people were really quite upset. I just had this experience with a professor who maybe wasn't sensitive to how some of us were feeling. Choices were made during the class that did not honor our emotional struggle. I talked with several students after the class and I sent her an email saying, "This is the experience that some of us had and are having on this day." She heard that and apologized to the class. We dialogued about it and I ended up developing more confidence in this professor. So those are some of the strategies that we can use. How do you go back to places like rural Georgia and have these conversations? You start with the people closest to you, which is hard. That's the hardest work I think.

SECTION IV:

—————————

CLOSING WORDS—
WHY YOUR LIBERATION IS BOUND UP WITH MINE

WHAT THE WORLD NEEDS NOW

by Jasmine Syedullah, PhD

The perception that human life has differential exchange value in the marketplace of death when it comes to "civilized" and "uncivilized" peoples is not only quite common in liberal democratic countries; it is necessary to a hierarchical global order.

—TALAL ASAD

Contrary to popular belief, in the United States, freedom is a prison.

The notion may strike the modern American imagination as counterintuitive, or just plain wrong. But if we turn to the language of the Constitution, we find this loophole, a glaring time warp of contradiction that legitimates the ongoing presence of slave-like conditions within our national practice of liberty. The Thirteenth Amendment, the Constitutional abolition of slavery in 1865, remains one of this country's crowning achievements, proof-positive that democracy works and is an ever-evolving, self-correcting system of consensus, justice, and deliberation. The Amendment states that "neither slavery nor involuntary servitude, *except as a punishment for crime* … shall exist within the United States, or any place subject to their jurisdiction" (emphasis added by author).

I could not have arrived at this insight alone. My thinking on freedom is benefited by a groundswell of literatures by courageous and powerful activist scholars including Ruth Wilson Gilmore, Dennis Childs, Heather Ann Thompson, Dylan Rodriguez, Andrea Smith, Cheryl Harris, Joy James, and, of course, Angela Davis. Even by its own reckoning, the Federal Bureau of Prisons has determined that only three percent of the people put in prison are there as a result of homicide, aggravated assault, or kidnapping offenses. Despite the fact that one in three adult women and one in ten men are the reported survivors of sexual assault in this country, less than eight percent of federal prisoners are incarcerated for crimes of sexual violence. This is not to say we should be locking up more people, but just to show that the vast majority of those living behind bars are there for reasons associated with the possession of drugs and crimes of poverty.

Unlike the slave, the modern-day criminal is not only identified by markers of race—her presence poses a problem to common-sense understandings of public safety for a number of race-related reasons. She could present an undesirable economic status, state of indebtedness, affiliation of religious faith, unconventional performance of gender. She could be a problem on account of her lack of access to mental or physical health, education, employment, or shelter. Justifications for criminalization and incarceration are symbiotically connected to conditions of despotism, dispossession, and disenfranchisement that long precede the forcible migration of free people into prison. They are rooted in the injustices of liberal individualism and the exploitation of a vampiric capitalist system of wealth accumulation. The reality of American freedom is that it requires that many of us remain captive to preserve the illusion of freedom for all. As *The Guardian* reported in an article titled "A Tale of Two Tyras" in January 2016, it is a national ideal that ensures "one out of every 110 adult Americans lives under the lock and key."

In other words, the kinds of captivity the abolition of slavery consecrated in the crucible of that peculiar institution are now condoned in an exercise in dehumanization that is based on, but far greater than, the historical scale and scope of anti-Black racism. It is a practice of freedom rooted in the historical logics and civilizing rationalizations for slavery, but, thanks to the Constitutional victory of 1865, it extends this peculiar logic beyond the policing of the perimeters of Blackness to all those who fall within reach of U.S. Empire and its peace keeping missions. The practices of convict leasing, segregation, racial profiling, stop and frisk, and extraordinary rendition extend from Leavenworth, to Attica, and from Guantanamo to culminate in the indiscriminate use of mass criminalization—the proliferation of prisons and prison-like conditions designed to keep "us" safe.

Ever since the loophole of the Thirteenth Amendment empowered the United States to democratize the experience of captivity far beyond the color line, far beyond the physical space of the prison, the United States of America has become the planet's largest jailer, representing almost one-quarter of the world's total prison population. As much as we want to believe in the promise of the American dream, the complete autonomy of the nuclear family, the domestic privacy of home ownership, the protections of our private property from the interference of the national government in our everyday lives, this halcyon wholesome image of freedom is only thinkable because of the fictions we spin around it. It is, in reality, a thing rendered unfathomable for a large population of those this country seeks to protect.

We need to dismiss as pretense, then, that the freedom abolition won can protect us from de-territorialization, slave labor, lynch culture, legal segregation, forced encampment, home invasions, terrorism, or death, i.e., becoming disposable. What I would like to propose in these closing words is that *what we need now is not more freedoms but more fugitives!* We needed fugitives to find the loopholes in our *language of* **liberation.** We need fugitives now to keep abolishing the legacies of slavery, colonialism, and genocide that persist in the present day. What the world needs now is a pursuit of freedom rooted not in fear of someone "taking" what's "ours," but in a radical kind of love that refuses to settle for meanings of justice, safety, and independence that re-create the shackles, borders, color lines, and other punitive forms of policing and surveillance we just escaped to claim our freedom. Our imaginations of freedom have to be born out of a practice of inhabiting places of containment with an improbable sense of unity, compassion, conviction, and possibility.

Rather than envision freedom as our inoculation from difference, as freedom from a collective commitment to those still in bondage, I am interested in how we can make possible a new politics of friendship, a new practice of the political, a new way of being together in which we can imagine the value of freedom anew, not as an abstract set of ideals that conceal the consequence of our freedoms, but as a practice of mutual respect, reconciliation, and repair through which our communities might heal from the injury American freedoms have exacted upon our bodies. No, not just for one. What we need now are sweet ways for everyone to remain fugitive within the domain of state-sanctioned violence and neglect that would otherwise render our lives immaterial.

RADICAL PRESENCE

by Lama Rod Owens

*I like to arrive 10 minutes early just to let bitches know who
the f**k they dealin' wit*

—RuPaul

If I can't dance, I don't want to be part of your revolution.

—Emma Goldman

*There is a candle in your heart, ready to be kindled.
There is a void in your soul, ready to be filled.
You feel it, don't you?*

—Rumi

*The secret doctrine nonsense: it's secret because no one under-
stands it. When they think they do, that's when things really
go awry. In reality, nothing is hidden. The whole point is that
it's there always. But we have to uncover the wisdom that is.*

—Karma Wangmo

A friend admitted during her introduction before one of my
dharma talks that I had intrigued her because she had never
heard a dharma teacher say the things I did during teachings.
I was tickled because she was right, and this is a very common
feedback I receive.

Over the past several years of being a formal dharma teacher, my style of teaching has evolved to be a very informal and what seems to be an unorganized flow of thoughts, impressions, insights, and direct references to pop-culture happenings. I almost never prepare written notes, and even if I have already selected a topic and teaching description, I often have no idea what I will be saying on the topic until I sit on the cushion and open my mouth. I know that this scares the shit out of people. I noticed that when I prepared a dharma talk, I was expecting people to show up and meet me where I was. This began to feel a little manipulative and insensitive to the needs of folks in the space. Unconsciously, my goal became to meet people where they are in the very moment we begin to share space together. I do not know where the group is until I am in the group. I can write a dharma talk beforehand, but that talk is based upon where I think the group will be at the time of the talk and therefore doesn't take into consideration the unique causes and conditions that inform how individuals are showing up in that moment and how that particular showing up has to be seen, appreciated, and spoken to. Overall, I just try to trust where I am led.

In my tradition, it is customary to recite a lineage prayer before offering a teaching. The lineage prayer connects us to the blessings of the great masters who have come before us and reminds us that we are a vessel transmitting the precious and sacred teachings that have been passed down in an unbroken line since the historical Buddha. My practice is not so much a formal prayer but an acknowledgement that I am not alone, that there have been a multitude of beings that have conspired to place me in my dharma.

Not only do I lean into my lineage, I am surrendering to Tara, the female Buddha associated with compassion, a figure that I am currently relating to as my personal deity. Tara, or any Buddha for that matter, is not separate from myself, but arises from within my consciousness as a reflection of my own innate compassion, concern, and deep sensitivity. She reminds me that this body, my body, that has shown up to transmit dharma, has earned this dharma through developing an intimate relationship with suffering and has been chosen for this suffering to be a teacher guiding others toward liberation. When I am surrendering to Tara, I am asking the precious woman to hold my hand.

I have come to think of the way I show up as a dharma teacher as an expression of radical presence. Radical presence is being in the world, taking up space, and loving myself without apology. As a dharma teacher, radical presence means that I am allowing dharma to manifest through me as I am situated in my particular intersectionality as a Black, queer, cisgendered, enabled-bodied male, who is mixed-classed and radically minded.

There is a distrust of identity in dharma communities. Part of this distrust is an authentic desire to transcend ego-based identifications that keep us rooted in dualistic suffering. However, most often I experience this distrust as a strategy to control and gain power over who has a right to talk about dharma in spaces and how dharma is talked about. When bodies are controlled, then there is less chance that the dominant group will be made uncomfortable having to tolerate a dharma expression that reminds them of their implicit role in the suffering of underrepresented groups.

When I am able to walk in the door embracing all aspects of my intersectional identity while allowing myself the grace to teach through my identity, I am transmitting a dharma from my experience of being at home in my body, where I am least likely to reproduce psychic violence, by offering dharma through a mind that denies and rejects vital parts of myself. When I am not aware of my difference, I am not aware of yours, and therefore I share a dharma that does not see you as you are, conferring a kind of judgment that says that part of you is not welcomed in this space and that thus becomes violent. This is the experience of folks from oppressed communities in *sanghas* right now.

Radical presence is the practice of authenticity, which is the practice of staying true to one's self. It implies that what we say or do is in accord with our truest desires and aspirations. In my experience, authenticity is about embracing my unique personality as it manifests in the world. It is about recognizing that my experience has been shaped and will continue to be shaped by the communities that I have been raised in. There is sensitivity to the pressure from dharma communities and society in general to conform in certain ways that may or may not be conducive to my overall health and well-being. Authenticity is the conscious choice to be true to my own experience and the struggle of being attentive and patient with how my experience has been shaped through factors both in and out of my control. It is not an easy practice. It requires a certain level of confidence and trust in my experience as something that is valuable and meaningful.

Radical presence is recognizing the particular locations and intersections of identity we occupy and connecting to others through these identities. I try to model that it is possible to be both Buddhist and queer and Black and radical. I try to model what it looks like to have an integrated teaching of honoring these identities and striving to benefit others through Dharma practice.

This is what authenticity calls me to do. It helps me remain present to what others are feeling because I am present to my own situation. It can be uncomfortable and lonely. Yet at the end of the day, I feel as if this place of being uncomfortable is where I am still growing as a dharma teacher.

What we experience in spaces dominated by white supremacist cultural normalization and/or the supremacy of the Asian culture as the origin of our tradition is a kind of exclusivity that problematizes the authentic expression of those of us not members of one of these groups. What I experience is being in places where I feel there is no space or consideration for how social oppression colors the way I need dharma to be transmitted. This transmission must be an interrogation of the ways oppression is reproduced in *sanghas* when the groups most responsible for systematic oppression continue to dominate. When queer bodies, or female bodies, or other kinds of marginalized bodies, are not represented, then what is left is a space that reproduces the psychic violence of silencing, ignoring, and othering.

I do the things that I do because I know that I can die at any second. I experience great suffering when I forget my impermanence. My teachers have taught me to love myself, and that has caused me to love beings in the world. There is no greater work than the work of self-love because that lies at the heart of our liberation from ignorance. I show up because of love. I am present because of love. I am alive because of love. I thrive because I am loved. Radical presence is born out of love.

In the end, may all beings be liberated through the celebration and love of the things we all once suffered from.

A NEW DHARMA: PROPHETIC WISDOM AND THE RISE OF TRANSCENDENT MOVEMENTS

by Rev. angel Kyodo williams, Sensei

Black Prophetic Fire is simply a way of saying … we need a renaissance of integrity, courage, vision, willingness to serve and, most importantly, willingness to sacrifice.

—CORNEL WEST

My question's always how do we regain that kind of vision and that prophetic vision? That fire … to use the words of Professor Cornel West, that prophetic Black tradition? How do we return to that in a way that's not materialistic or self-serving?

—LAMA ROD OWENS, RADICAL DHARMA CONVERSATIONS, ATLANTA, GA

THE VOICE OF PROPHETIC WISDOM

Much has been said about the loss of the prophetic tradition, particularly the Black prophetic voice, post–civil rights. In effect, the signing of the Civil Rights Act in 1964 exchanged the false promise of equality for Black people for a muzzle on the voices of those who would continue to challenge white supremacy and its manifestations.

The voice that would continue to shout America awake from the sleepwalking that perpetuates the status quo of capitalism, militarism, exceptionalism, and colonialism has been silenced to gain access to vestiges of power, middle-class privileges, occasional material success stories, and rarified entry into the pearly gates of fame.

People who disrupt the American dream–state by laying bare the connection of the cancer of multinational corporate capitalism to the theft of indigenous and first-nation lands, the genocide of their people, the struggles of the poor in Latin America, the starvation of sub-Saharan Africa, the mass incarceration of Palestinians, the displacement of Middle Easterners, and the disruption of the climate in a habitat known to us as earth have been few in number.

A NEW DHARMA

With the exception of Malcolm X, the Black prophetic voice has been erringly associated with Christianity. The prophets called for in these times necessarily arise from, to paraphrase Dr. Ibrahim Farajajé, organic (post, trans, and) multi-religiosity.

Prophetic wisdom, while likely drawing on the particular religious and spiritual inspiration of its conveyor, transcends dualism or any frames that would limit the creative emergence of truth. Rather than adherence to or containment by particular ideology, its starting point is that fundamental wisdom and basic goodness are inherent. As a result, it pivots away from salvation toward liberation. Not "liberation from," which mirrors salvation, but rather "liberation for the sake of it," which presupposes that it is always there.

Collectively, its practitioners are bound by an allegiance to what I refer to as a new dharma. It is an approach rather than a method. Dynamic, rather than static. Emergent, rather than pre-conceived. A how, rather than a what. It is the way in which dharma—universal truth—embedded within and across wisdom traditions, whether east, west, indigenous, ancient, tribal, or revealed, expresses itself in this culture in this moment of time.

Dharma is a Sanskrit word meaning universal truth, teachings, that which is firm, living in accordance with natural order, among other things. The religions that have historically been associated with it date back over five thousand years. Though it should be noted that while they are often referred to as the oldest, they are practically new compared with the collective religions of ethnic indigenous peoples.

New dharma embraces the mash-up of those ancient teachings coming into contact with traditional Western religions, and earth-based spiritualities.

- like the dharmic religions, time is held as fundamentally cyclical, but
- like the Abrahamic religions, attends to linear
- like indigenous and earth-based religions, dharma respects the sacredness of the earth and all its manifestations and seeks to remember our right relationship with it
- like the Vedantic, it pursues liberation from cycles of suffering (minimally, in this lifetime)
- like Judaism, it embraces the mending of the world
- like the path of Buddha, it is based in self-discovery, rather than strict adherence to belief
- like Jainism, all of life is sacred
- like the path of Jesus, love is front and center

• like Baha'i, it acknowledges unity in diversity: all humanity created as equals with appreciation and acceptance of the diversity of all races and cultures

New dharma also integrates emerging fields of study that draw heavily across traditions, theories, methodologies, pedagogies, and practices. It is willing to embrace the revelations of new sciences while recognizing they are only revealing what has always been known by peoples and wisdoms since lost or never validated within the narrow scope of Western ontology. Most notable are embodied cognition, somatic lenses, brain science, and all praxes seeking to reunite the mind-body complex in an act of insurgence against the disembodied culture that is a direct outcome of white supremacy and mass oppression.

So, whether they reveal themselves as spiritual warriors, humanistic soldiers, yogic guerillas, political organizers, religious idealists, intellectual theorists, creative luminaries, cultural technicians, architects of the sacred, protectors of the mundane, they are all modern-day prophets. Wisdom prophets who lay bare the unarmed truth of the transgenerational cultural illness of white superiority in equal measure with an unapologetic love that holds those besieged by that plague in the light of their humanity, distinguishing disease from host, are being called forth ... and they are gaining in number.

POSSIBILITY, PRESENCE, POWER, PEOPLE

As is the case with any prophetic instrument, practitioners must cultivate an interiority, an attention to the inner life that unhooks overdependency on external sources of validation. Awareness—reflective and contemplative practices that turn attention inward—converts self-inquiry into a welcome opportunity rather than a threat. It exposes unvarnished aspects of your self, which may give you the opportunity to work it into a shine. Most importantly, though, when you allow your practice to be one of bearing witness to suffering, opening yourself to not knowing, you directly cultivate compassion from wise action.

Some examples of how to accomplish such awareness include:

- time in nature
- focused thought
- centering prayer
- movement practices
- mindfulness
- Shamatha/Vipassana meditation
- just sitting
- other forms of meditation

See the following for more information: www.contemplative mind.org/practices/tree.

A steady mind is a mind empowered to see more clearly what is being called for and relieves the prophet from an unsustainable, externally motivated drive to do. It provides the container in which to contemplate the questions posed by W. E. B. Du Bois, paraphrased by Cornel West, that prophets must search for responses to ceaselessly: *"How does integrity face oppression? What shall honesty do in the face of deception? What does decency do in the face of insult? And how does virtue meet brute force?"*[5]

A rich relationship with one's inner life deepens the root of integrity, fortifies the heart of courage, sharpens the eye of vision, and strengthens the will to serve and the resolve to sacrifice.

This all may seem contradictory to the vigorous pursuit of leadership by the "Cs": collaboration, collective, and community. Nevertheless, it is a path to appropriate balance between abdication to the messianic one and capitulation to the tyrannical many. That said, leaders and prophets may not be one and the same, though they both function on behalf of the people. "The people" must always mean having the voices and needs of the oppressed, disenfranchised, marginalized, underserved, subjugated, and silenced as its center. While they may have hailed from the margins, leaders often draw their power from the center and then stand out in front, that others might emulate—both a gift and a curse. Prophets always insist that the mainstream extend to the margins—which they live among and speak from—rather than trying to "bring them in," which only relocates who is in and who is out, once again leaving an elite few to decide.

They do this often at great cost—even to life and liberty—because, by remaining a constant pole signaling what and who remains on the outside, which reminds us of the work undone, they pose a threat to the effort of anyone who would paper over truth as a pretense of peace. Including, sometimes, that of movement leaders.

---

[5] "Black Prophetic Fire: Cornel West on the Revolutionary Legacy of Leading African-American Voices," interview by Amy Goodman, *Democracy Now!* October 6, 2014.

Prophets must be multi-disciplinary, culturally aware, socially translingual, mentally stable, emotionally intelligent, ideologically flexible, and ethically integral. They must be fierce believers in possibility, rigorous cultivators of presence, effective wielders of power, and ardent lovers of people. They must endeavor, at all costs, to establish and maintain the aspiration to be free. They must love the whole of life so completely that they embody joy in the face of suffering. Indeed, they know them to be two faces of the one lover. They must, for the sake of us all and despite external conditions that would dictate the contrary, learn how to live and be and become a liberated life.

This insurgence of prophetic wisdom is both a forecast and organic byproduct of those newly inhabited ways of achieving social change. Transformative, radical, interconnected, and embodied. Ways that are motivated by a deep, unwavering love of all of life, and committed to seeing that love expressed as justice.

INTERCONNECTEDNESS

Beloved community is formed not by the eradication of difference but by its affirmation, by each of us claiming the identities and cultural legacies that shape who we are and how we live in the world.

—BELL HOOKS, *KILLING RAGE: ENDING RACISM*

In addition to the realization of our interdependence—mutuality—glimpses of interconnectedness are powerful because they open a window into a possibility that heretofore we were unaware of. These glimpses into *oneness* shed a light and invigorate a hope that I think we all come in with, but our experience of life and our wrong view of life starts to beat us down. We stop even hoping for the possibility of profound peace. We tell ourselves "it's just a pipe dream. The closest I might get is to stop having my people gunned down on the streets by the police." If that's all there is, mere survival, we lose hope.

Of course, we need the immediate cessation of being under siege. This experience of being under siege makes for a life that is intolerable. If our movements focus solely on rights (as if there were wrongs, as if there were human beings—species even—that are not entitled to thrive by the mere fact of their existence), then that polarized view gives rise to the very policing that diminishes humanity by seeking to sort us into categories of relative entitlements. When we allow ourselves to operate inside of this framework, we abdicate our responsibility to fully engage each other as human beings. We give power over to a few people to qualify and quantify those categories of entitlement.

If we can't dream greater, we are only demanding lives that are just outside of intolerable. So these glimpses are an opportunity to tap into the hopefulness of certainty—which is profound, because it implies hopefulness not only for ourselves but also for our entire society. All is not lost.

The aspiration to liberation that is rooted in interconnectedness takes us somewhere else entirely different because it doesn't merely demand a right; it asserts Truth. Properly envisioned, liberation movements transport us into the position of asserting the undeniable truth of thriving as a human inevitability.

TRANSCENDENT MOVEMENTS

It has long been believed that you can only truly organize

people around issues that matter to them, but collective liberation asks something greater of us. It requires transcendent movements.

Transcendent movements require people to organize around issues beyond what people perceive they are affected by. How to do that? People have to experience their interdependence. To recognize that any limit in your ability to love limits my ability to love. One has to penetrate the truth of interdependence such that I am moved to a place in which I am not doing something for you, but it is actually about me, which is tied to you because there is, in an absolute sense, no separation.

imasmim sati, idam hoti.

imass uppada idam uppajjati.

imasmim asati, idam na hoti.

imassa nirodha, idam nirujjhati.

This being, that becomes;

from the arising of this, that arises;

this not being, that does not become;

from the ceasing of this, that ceases.[6]

---

[6] Oneness: Also referred to as the Nidāna ("basis" or "ground") doctrine. The historic Buddha taught both dependent origination and causality. It is the most often repeated phrase in the Buddhist Canon, appearing at least in these texts and possibly more: Majjhima-Nikaya i.263, ii.32, iii.63 Samyutta-Nikaya ii.28, 65, 70, 78, 79, 95, 96, v.388; (all references in Nidāna Samyutta.)

We have arrived in the era of what I call embodied intersectionality. Originally coined as a phrase in 1989 by attorney and critical theorist Kimberlé Crenshaw, the term intersectionality sought to give language to the ways in which Black women were often marginalized because they didn't fit in solely one category or another, and, given that different forms of discrimination can interact and overlap, sisters were often erased from advocacy by white feminists and male antiracists. It has since come into common usage in progressive and liberation movements to express the interconnectedness of various forms of oppression.

More than a political concept, embodied intersectionality is the lived reality of an increasing number of people crossing boundaries of race, class, gender, religion, sexual orientation, national citizenry, ethnic origin, etc., and the cultures formed by those identities and locations. It is a tangible, modern-day expression of oneness. The long-standing ways of tribalism and hyper-individualism are both fading from the mainstream, while at the same time are inciting reactivity in the form of greater political division. This is evidenced by the deeper and seemingly more vicious, rabid divide between the left and right, conservatives and progressives, Democrats and Republicans, and in fragmentation within those groups, as well.

So how to get there from here?

Intersectionality includes but goes beyond how we build vital bridges across what James Keen and his co-authors call "significant lines of difference." We have long known that our survival is tied up with each other's; as King said, "we are caught in an inescapable network of mutuality, tied in a single garment of destiny." But to actually be able to hold specific campaigns, projects, issues and movements within this imperative is a whole other story.[7]

LOTUS OUT OF THE MUD

Paradoxically, the individualist ethos handed down from America's terrible founding, as distinct from more collectivized/social-cultural organization (of the East, for example,) provides an opportunity to transmute that destructive force of aggression and narcissism to approach collective liberation from entirely new ways.

The two elements that most quicken the potential for transcendent movements are not entirely unique but are prominent features of American society:

1. embodied intersectionality
2. the entitlement of individualism

The depth and breadth of embodied intersectionality at a critical mass are the direct outcome of a non-homogenous society, the best example of which is the experiment called the United States of America and this admittedly accidental outcome.

It seems unlikely we could have truly envisioned collective liberation prior to intersectionality because we had so much cultural hegemony. I would go so far as to propose that even the idea of collective liberation expressed beyond the theoretical, as it is in the spiritual aspiration of the bodhisattva ideal, and instead rendered as a broad-based agenda for social justice, is a direct result of intersectionality.

---

[7] Claudia Horwitz, "The Spaces of Intersectionality," *Stone Circles* (blog), August 2012.

Intersectionality is its own ideal.

America in all its messiness provides for the first real opportunity for this because so many people are still in touch with their mother countries and mother cultures or are reclaiming cultural identities distinct from and against whiteness as the model of perfection.

In, as bell hooks says, "claiming the identities and cultural legacies that shape who we are and how we live in the world," we reject hegemony, the very thing that allows us to organize solely around similarities or simple tribalism. The impulse to assert our right to claim who we are is an essential human urge toward self-determination, but the comparative strength and relative speed by which we do so in America, overriding the drive to assimilate as the hegemonic order would have us do, is a direct byproduct of the individual sense of entitlement, perhaps inherited or borrowed from our contact with the privileged whom such entitlement was meant to be bestowed upon.

But even as we claim our identities, which could be seen as leading to self-centered ideologies or just cliquishness—perhaps an unavoidable developmental stage that critics of identity politics have pointed out—intersectionality incites us to reject internal cultural and identity hegemony.

The reason we can is the result of so many people—approaching a critical mass—living intersectional lives. Enough of us can feel beyond cosmetic sameness and experience the deeper interdependent relationship, moving the mutuality of liberation from theory to practice to praxis.

The greatest potential outcome of embodied intersectionality meets individual entitlement is transcendent movements.

EMBRACING WHAT IS, THROWING NOTHING AND NO ONE AWAY

These converging paradoxes are allowing for possibilities of human evolution that were not previously possible.

We may initially experience this paradox as something to be resisted because we are deeply invested in right and wrong. We want to cut things off, throw something away. But in a world of multiplicity, the path toward liberatory mastery—personal and social—can no longer remain rooted in a single ideology, discipline, or viewpoint; it itself is becoming intersectional and interdependent. Through practice, we can create the invitation to be in relationship with the reality of what is. Even when we disagree with it, if for no other reason than that our disagreement does not negate the reality.

Simultaneously with our commitment to disrupting and dismantling structures that degrade humanity, a commitment to the practice of engaging the humanity of people wed to perpetuating those structures must co-exist. Whether by arrogance, ignorance, or fear, we must bear witness to their suffering as our own. Challenge what is unjust. Invest in their basic goodness. Always moving toward integration. Without this commitment and practice, we merely mirror the destructive forces of polarization and power.

On the movement level, this allows for uplifted organizing at the highest common denominator rather than the degradation of lowest common denominator, which is a vastly different way of being with what is and with being present with those we might staunchly disagree with or oppose.

This is a huge evolutionary leap: to be able to see past sameness and likeness as the lens through which we view our potential to care for and love one another. We've done this on the individual level, but we are now organizing on the social level. In many ways this goes against—or extends beyond—the grain of how we have been evolving. Biologically speaking, we are programmed toward being tribal as a means of survival. We literally have to transcend an aspect of our own biology.

This ability to disrupt our programming and form new cognitive connections based on direct experience that then becomes embodied through repetition—practice—is one of human beings' greatest attributes. In this lies the potential to overcome our basest reactions for survival and manifest our highest evolutionary potential to thrive. It is profound, and it is possible, and we can see it.

May it be so.

Insha'allah

Svaha

Amen

Amin

Ache

Jai, Jai, Jai Mitra

GLOSSARY

Black liberation movement: Refers to specific movements in the United States that have focused on addressing the oppression of Black folks, including the civil rights movement, the Black Power movement, and the current Black Lives Matter movement.

Black Lives Matter: The current Black liberation movement founded by Alicia Garza, Patrisse Cullors, and Opal Tometi in response to the visible police violence against Black folks, in particular to the murder of Trayvon Martin. It is a movement that seeks to highlight the inherent devaluing of Black life while uplifting the valuable contributions of Black folks to this world.

bodhicitta: A Sanskrit word meaning the altruistic wish to achieve enlightenment to benefit others.

bodhisattva: A Sanskrit word that translates literally to "awake being." A Spiritual Warrior in Buddhism, it is like a saint who vows to achieve enlightenment only to free others. Many Buddhists take the Bodhisattva Vow in which they commit to spiritual enlightenment in this life and all lives to come in order to liberate others.

Buddha: Meaning the "Enlightened One." It is the name given to Shakyamuni after his enlightenment. However, all beings process Buddhanature and can become Buddhas after having reached the state of spiritual attainment where true nature of mind is recognized.

cisgender: Opposite of transgender. A person whose gender identity matches their sex at birth.

class maintenance: The specific ways in which folks maintain their class privilege through acts of oppression, manipulation, and other forms of violence.

compassion: The wish for others to be free from suffering or discomfort.

demon: A supernatural being that is not a god but more human.

Dharma/dharma: A Sanskrit word that has several meanings. The teachings of the Buddha usually appear as "the *Dharma;*" more generally, and in lowercase, it refers to "truth," "the law," or one's path in life. It is also a way to describe how things really are or the truth of reality. In this case, it is sometimes anglicized as Truth and appears as "*Dharma.*"

Four Noble Truths: The first sermon the Buddha delivered after his enlightenment that explains the truths: 1. That there is suffering in our lives. 2. That attachment lies at the heart of suffering. 3. That there is a way out of this suffering. 4. That the Eightfold Path is the strategy to liberate ourselves from suffering.

karma: A Sanskrit word meaning cause and effect. More specifically, it refers to action and the consequences of action.

lovingkindness meditation: Often called *metta* practice in Theravada traditions, it is the practice of deepening love and compassion for self and learning to extend love and compassion to others.

patriarchy: A system of power and dominance in which men are privileged. Patriarchy also refers to the strategies both men and women use to oppress women. According to bell hooks, patriarchy is not gendered.

race: According to People's Institute for Survival and Beyond (PISAB), a specious classification of human beings created by Europeans (whites), which assigns human worth and social status using "white" as the model of humanity and the height of human achievement for the purpose of establishing and maintaining privilege and power.

samsara: A Pali and Sanskrit word meaning the cycle of birth, life, and death and the karma associated with the perpetuation of this cycle until the illusion of the whole process is realized through practice. *Samsara* is also called an expression of ignorance.

sangha: Traditionally meaning the monastic community of Buddhist practitioners, now more contemporarily understood to be the community or congregation of Buddhist practitioners lay and ordained.

shamatha: In the Pali language of early Buddhist texts, *shamatha* means tranquility. It is often used to describe one of the two main categories of Buddhist meditation (the other being *vipassana,* or insight).

Three Jewels: The three foundations of Buddhist practice—the Buddha (the teacher), the *Dharma* (the law), and the *Sangha* (the spiritual community). They are also referred to as the Triple Gems.

tonglen: The practice of taking and sending or exchanging one's self for others; originates from the *lojong* (mind training) teachings of Tibetan Buddhism.

transgender: Opposite of cisgender. A person whose gender identity does not match their sex at birth.

violence: the physical or emotional force against another's will.

vipassana: In the Pali language of the early Buddhist texts, *vipassana* means insight. It is often used to describe one of the two main categories of Buddhist meditation (the other being *shamatha,* or tranquility).Vipassana also refers to the tradition in the West also known as Insight Meditation.

white privilege: According to Sharon Martinas, a historically based, institutionally perpetuated system of preferential prejudice for and treatment of white people based solely on their skin color and/or ancestral origin from Europe.

white supremacy: According to white anti-racist trainers Mickey Ellinger and Sharon Martinas, a historically based, institutionally perpetuated system of exploitation and oppression of continents, nations, and peoples of color by white peoples and nations of the European continent for the purpose of establishing, maintaining, and defending a system of wealth, power, and privilege.

wisdom: Traditionally, the state of clearly understanding the nature of reality. In a more contemporary sense, it is relating to relationships, situations, and reality with clarity and insight into how these things are functioning in such a way that suffering is decreased.

zendo: In Zen Buddhism, a "meditation hall" where zazen (formal meditation) practice is done.

ABOUT THE AUTHORS

Called "the most intriguing (and vocal) African-American Buddhist" by *Library Journal,* **angel Kyodo williams** is an author, activist, master trainer, and founder of the Center for Transformative Change. She has been bridging the worlds of transformation and justice since her critically acclaimed book, *Being Black: Zen and the Art of Living With Fearlessness and Grace* was hailed as "an act of love" by Pulitzer Prize winner Alice Walker, and "a classic" by Buddhist pioneer Jack Kornfield. She is second of only three black women Zen "Senseis" or teachers. She applies wisdom teachings and embodied practice to intractable social justice issues and is a preeminent thought leader of Transformative Social Change. In recognition of her work, angel received one of the first Creating Enlightened Society Awards from Sakyong Mipham Rinpoche, the leader of the Shambhala tradition. Her work has been widely covered, including in T*he New York Times, Washington Post, Boston Globe, Buddhadharma, Lion's Roar, Ms.,* and *Essence.* angel notes, "Love and Justice are not two. Without inner change, there can be no outer change. Without collective change, no change matters."

http://angelkyodowilliams.com

Photo © Erica Camille

Lama Rod Owens is an activist/organizer, poet, and graduate of the traditional three-year retreat program at Kagyu Thubten Choling Monastery, where he received his teaching authorization from his root teacher, the Venerable Lama Norlha Rinpoche in the Tibetan tradition of Buddhism. He is a core teacher with Natural Dharma Fellowship in Cambridge, Massachusetts, and is also a graduate student in Buddhist Studies at Harvard Divinity School. Lama Rod is interested in the intersection of Buddhism, identity, and social change. Known for his informal teaching style rooted in self-inquiry and humor, he has appeared in the Buddhist publications *Lion's Roar* and *Buddhadharma* and has been recognized as one of the emerging leaders of the next generation of Dharma teachers.

Photo © Megan Pearse

Jasmine Syedullah holds a PhD in politics with a designated emphasis in feminist studies and history of consciousness from University of California, Santa Cruz, and a BA from Brown University in religious studies with a focus in Buddhist philosophy. Syedullah is currently a University of California President's Postdoctoral Fellow and lectures on her work at colleges and universities throughout the country. She has a sixteen-year-long meditation practice and has been sitting at the feet of Rev. angel Kyodo williams since 2004.

ACKNOWLEDGMENTS

JASMINE SYEDULLAH

Invitation to collaborate on this project could not have arrived in my life at a more auspicious moment. It has buffered my transition from graduate school to whatever comes next in ways that have made it possible to imagine my future at a place that has prepared for me to bring my whole self to the table. For this and for leading in ways that take care of those who will come behind, I am immensely grateful for the forethought of Rev. angel and Lama Rod in seeing fit to include me in these incredible conversations. I am also deeply indebted to my faithful editor and platonic life partner Olivia Ford for helping me see what I mean to say before I even think it; to my dharmasister Emily O'Dell for reading early versions of my essays and seeding the wonderful conversations that give them life; and to our project transcription editor and my sangha sister *Simha* Evan Stubblefield for her careful eye, skillful ear, and back in a flash turn-around. During the rapid fire evolution of this project from transcriptions to chapters to manuscript I found refuge, contemplative space, and much needed live jazz and punk rock music breaks staying with my dear friend and fellow academic activist Jenny Hubbard, whose heated pool, grill-ready deck, and brilliant creative mind provided much sustenance for long nights and days of writing, brainstorming, and rewriting.

RADICAL DHARMA

Behind the scenes, the Radical Dharma team would not have been able to pull off this miracle without the administrative and moral support of Erica Śvani Grevemeyer, Valerie Moon, Taylor Jewel Devarie, and Cherisse Harper. In the field, I was inspired and impressed by the welcome and warmth of reception we received at our host sites in Atlanta, Brooklyn, Boston, and Berkeley. I would like to specifically extend deep gratitude to the beloved communities at Atlanta Shambhala Center, Charis Books, Brooklyn Zen Center, Harvard Divinity School, and the Center for Transformative Change, especially Daniel Phillips, Elizabeth Anderson, Greg Snyder, and Erika Carlsen. A huge thank you also to all those who helped us on location to navigate the local terrain of our host cities, bright among them Jamie M. Green-Fergerson, Pamela Ayo Yetunde, and last but never least, Danielle St. Louis.

LAMA ROD OWENS

First I offer thanks to my Dharma teachers for their extreme kindness in sharing the Dharma with me. I am thankful for the comradeship of Rev. angel Kyodo williams and Dr. Jasmine Syedullah. I thank Kathe McKenna for her mentorship and example of an uncompromising integration of dharma and justice. I thank my professors and friends Mark Jordan and Cheryl Giles for their constant support and encouragement. I thank the entire Harvard Divinity School community especially the Harvard Buddhist Community for their support. And lastly, I thank my mama, Wendy Owens, for being the first radical I ever knew.

212

ANGEL KYODO WILLIAMS

First and foremost, I express my gratitude to the ancestors, whether embodied in human, animal, plant or spirit form, who have entrusted me with the opportunity to carry the life-force of breath. I feel them in the oceans and forests, see them in the city streets and in the sunlight that glints against the flowing rivers.

My humble gratitude to my coauthors for your trust. I knew y'all were badass. No other two people would do. I love you both immeasurably. I am grateful for my parents, my teachers, my immediate and extended family, and for the new Dharma Community in all its permutations in the past fifteen years. Without each and every one of you, I would not know of a radical dharma, nor be inspired to express it. Karen Muktayani Villanueva has been a stabilizing force, whether near or far, over time. Valerie Moon has, for me personally, been a necessary buffer, a steady support, a second pair of sharp eyes, and made sure I knew where I needed to be since she arrived to assist me.

Gratitude to all the folks at North Atlantic Books, especially Tim McKee who had the willingness to take a risk so this book could be as responsive to the times and the community as possible. Hisae Matsuda and Ebonie Ledbetter ushered the process along. Bevin Donahue has been especially responsive to our promotion needs. Without Istanbul, my second city, which carries the spirit of James Baldwin, and likewise has provided me with a sense of space to turn back and look at my homeland with fresh eyes, this work would not have come to fruition. Zaza Prayer has been the anchor of my home there. I am grateful for his friendship and kindness.

This book is for all the people who have and continue to put the pursuit of liberation for all peoples and our planet above and beyond false notions of divisions by race, color, gender, creed, ethnic origin, or who one chooses to love. It recognizes the vast potential of the dharma. It celebrates the prophetic wisdom voiced throughout time and traditions. It honors the insistence for our collective dignity and freedom. It is for the love of black peoples everywhere.

There are too many people to capture here with any sense of satisfaction. If you are reading this, I am grateful for you, too. And you are loved.